Becoming More Like Christ

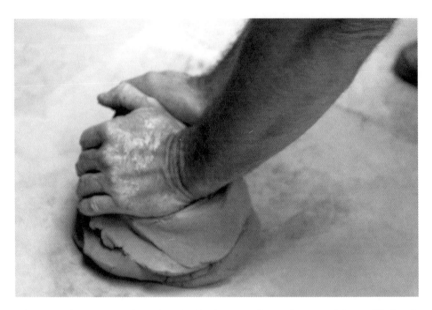

The image shows a potter kneading the clay in a very firm and purposeful way. The hands are pressing down on the clay from above and one can see that the job is unfinished and, at times, difficult. Experiencing Christ being formed in us is a hard, uncomfortable and sometimes painful process.

Becoming More Like Christ

A Contemporary Biblical Journey

DISCIPLESHIP AS WHOLENESS
VOLUME TWO

Peter R. Holmes
Susan B. Williams

LONDON • COLORADO SPRINGS • HYDERABAD

13 12 11 10 09 08 07   7 6 5 4 3 2 1

First published 2007 by Authentic Media
9 Holdom Avenue, Bletchley, Milton Keynes, Bucks, MK1 1QR, UK
1820 Jet Stream Drive, Colorado Springs, CO 80921, USA
OM Authentic Media, Medchal Road, Jeedimetla Village,
Secunderabad 500 055, A.P., India

www.authenticmedia.co.uk

Authentic Media is a division of IBS-STL U.K., limited by guarantee, with its
Registered Office at Kingstown Broadway, Carlisle, Cumbria CA3 0HA.
Registered in England and Wales No. 1216232. Registered charity 270162.

British Library Cataloguing in Publication Data
A catalogue record for this book is available from the British Library

ISBN-13: 978-1-84227-543-6
ISBN-10: 1-84227-543-7

Cover Design by fourninezero design.
Typesetting by Waverley Typesetters, Fakenham
Print Management by Adare Carwin
Printed and bound in Great Britain by J.H. Haynes & Co., Sparkford

To Albert and Edith Cooper
London City Missioners
who first introduced me (Peter) to Christ on earth
(The late 1950's – 1960's)

Contents

Preface   xiii

Introduction   xv
    Introducing the Series   xvi
    Introducing this Book   xviii
    And Finally ...   xix

1. Christ-Likeness?   1
    Introducing Christ-Likeness   3
    Christ as Role Model   5
    Christian Virtues   7
    In Summary   8
    Qualities of Christ-Likeness: Introduction   10

2. Some Thorny Issues   13
    New Creations?   13
    Finding a Balance   15
    So How Much Can We Do?   16
    In Summary   19
    Qualities of Christ-Likeness: Your View of Yourself   21

3. The Challenge: Defining Christian Maturity   26
    Maturity in Christ in Scripture   26
    Maturity in Contemporary Psychology   28
    Contemporary Christian Maturity   30
    In Summary   32
    Qualities of Christ-Likeness: Your Character and
    Nature   36

4. Change and Christ-Likeness   42
      The Early Church and Personal Change   42
         The Importance of a Felt Faith   44
         Rethinking Christian Discipleship   45
         Change Separated from Learning   48
      In Summary   50

   Qualities of Christ-Likeness: Your Goals and Experience   52

5. Christ-Likeness: Becoming More Human?   57
      What Christ-Likeness Is Not   57
      Christ-Likeness Is Becoming More Human   58
      Christ-Likeness as Personal Uniqueness   60
      Christ-Likeness as Being Relational   62
      Social Intelligence   63
      Christ-Likeness as Continually Transformative   64
      Christ-Likeness Is Christ in Us   66
      In Summary   67

   Qualities of Christ-Likeness: Relationship with God   69

6. Christ-Likeness as Wholeness   74
      Christ-Likeness as Becoming More Whole   75
      "Therapeutic" Change, Christ-Likeness and
         Discipleship   78
      What Does This Christ-Like Journey Now Look
         Like?   80
      Taking Personal Responsibility   81
      Our View of Christ-Likeness   84

   Qualities of Christ-Likeness: Your Relationships with
      Others   87

7. Our Human Search for Authentic Spirituality   92
      Introducing Spiritual Reality   92
      Defining Spirituality   94
      Introducing Contemporary Spirituality   96
      Where Is This Transforming Spirituality in the
         Church?   98
      Spiritual Gifts from God   99

   Qualities of Christ-Likeness: Our Spirituality   103

8. Obstacles to Becoming Christ-Like   107
    A Hebrew View of Sin and Repentance   107
    Sin and Wholeness   110
    Recovering a Lost Language   111
    In Summary   113
    Qualities of Christ-Likeness: Our Intellectual Life   116

9. The Darkness in All of Us   119
    So What about Human Nature?   119
    A Tendency toward Self-Deception   121
    Naming Our Baggage   123
    What Baggage and Sin Have I Got?   124
    In Summary   126
    Qualities of Christ-Likeness: Family and Home 128

10. A Journey toward Christ-Likeness: How It Might Work
    for You   132
    Our Spiritual House   132
    Taking Possession of Our House: A Meditation   134
    "Feeling Is Healing"   137
    Human Emotion: God's Second Chance for Us   138
    What Your Journey Could Look Like   139
    In Summary   141
    Qualities of Christ-Likeness: The World   143

11. "Christ in Me?"   146
    What Does "Christ in Me" Really Mean?   147
    What Then Is Our Task?   148

Bibliography   150

Author Index   161

Scripture Index   164

Subject Index   167

None of us is born Christ-like.

None of us becomes Christ-like at conversion.

None of us becomes more Christ-like

by just being in church, or reading the Bible ...

We all need to change personally to become more like Jesus.

Preface

When Peter first invited me to co-author this book with him, the idea felt incongruous. How could I write anything about Christ-likeness?

I could understand Peter writing the book. From the first few days of knowing him I found myself deeply envious of his relationship with God. He had an unwavering single-minded focus on obedience to Christ that has remained unchanged to this day. His years of fasting, his capacity to hear the voice of God, his intimate knowledge of Scripture and theology – all these are reflected in this book. His self-discipline and capacity to love others in a selfless way without expecting anything back are familiar to those who have had the privilege of knowing him. But more than anything else, there is his love for Christ and it is this, embedded in every page, that makes this book what it is.

I would love to be able to claim that my own life has been full of such a hunger for Christ-likeness. But the truth is quite different. My relationship with God has been motivated more by a desperate need to recover from the cumulative impact of historic damage, and to help others do the same, than by love for Christ.[1] The healing and wholeness I have found are unapologetically miraculous, but fall far short of the Christ-likeness to which I aspire.

Nonetheless, when Peter gave me the first draft of the book to look at, I had to admit to a deep desire to make a contribution and share in its authorship. How many books on Christ-likeness do you know that have been written for women as well as men? And how many have been helpful to those like me, whose history would preclude them from a place in the Church, other than perhaps on the fringes or on the sick list? Where are the books that integrate the day-to-day practice and growth of Christ-likeness with Scripture and the rich historic and theological legacy of so many writers? And where will you find a meditation included offering a pathway to meet Christ in deeper intimacy? In co-authoring this book, Peter and I are aware that we have a greater opportunity to blend these perspectives on becoming more like Christ.

Come and join us on a journey into greater Christ-likeness, a journey that combines the sovereign work of God with personal commitment to ongoing positive change – a journey bringing deepening knowledge and experience of maturity in Christ. It is a journey for the young believer and the not-so-young, for the wealthy and the poor, for those with exceptionally damaged pasts and those who simply yearn for more of Christ. It is a journey for the Body of Christ.

SUSAN B. WILLIAMS
Life Giving Trust,
Deal, Kent, UK
January 2007

Introduction

Christianity has preached a gospel of salvation for hundreds of years. It has had huge success. But the salvation it has taught has often emphasized our destination after we die – heaven or hell. Today an additional emphasis would be helpful. We should be preaching and living the *whole* gospel.

Salvation is holistic: it is more than going to heaven, and the message of salvation is more than the story of how we can get there. Eternal life in heaven is part of the promise of God, but salvation is also about living in the Kingdom of God every day of this life on earth. Rather than being confined merely to churchgoing, salvation must bring personal and relational transformation here and now. The acceptance of salvation in Christ should change every aspect of our daily life. Salvation *now* means our becoming more Christ-like *now*, not just when we get to heaven.

Any presentation of the gospel, therefore, must include a *journey* toward greater Christ-likeness. In the Early Church this was assumed, as we will be noting later, but for many today it seems to have been separated from the idea of salvation. In this book we intend to outline the simple idea that the gospel message of salvation includes not only an initial experience of being saved, but also the need for all of us to go on a personal journey toward greater Christ-likeness.

We also intend to take this idea further. We will be suggesting that this journey has several aspects, including our becoming more human, more mature, more whole and a lot more competent in valuing relationships. In essence, the journey toward greater Christ-likeness in this life is part of the fulfillment of salvation. For instance, it means we find Love as God intended we should know and experience it.[2] We will therefore be describing salvation in part as a growing capacity to be more like Christ during our lifetime, incorporating a developing ability to love ourselves, others, the created world, and God as God.

As Christians we all celebrate miraculous change when it happens in ourselves and in others – note, for instance, the popularity of the Christian biography and autobiography. But we seem to devote pitifully little time to understanding how *we* might achieve this significant change. We often treat it as a sovereign work of God that mysteriously comes to some and not to others. Yet at the heart of Christianity is the duty to become more like Christ. It is the essence of discipleship, pastoral care and the journey toward greater sanctification. Every one of us needs to change in positive ways to become more like Jesus. We do not become more like Christ simply by using the correct words, going to church, or living by the Church's[3] rules. The Pharisees did all of these. More is needed, and this book will outline a discipleship wholeness journey that will help you both learn about and become more like Christ in every area of your life.

Introducing the Series

This is the second volume of three books. In 2005 I (Peter) wrote *Becoming More Human: Exploring the interface of spirituality, discipleship and therapeutic faith community*, which was the culmination of many years of reading and research.[4] This rather academic book is now being expanded into a series that unpacks its themes in greater detail. In the first volume, *Trinity in Human Community: Exploring congregational life in the image of the Social Trinity*,[5] I draw from both Susan's and my research to outline what can happen in a positive way to a congregation when it begins taking seriously the teachings of the Cappadocian Fathers. It was these Fathers who introduced the idea of the Trinity as a divine community. Writing in the fourth century, they reinstated neglected aspects of Biblical teaching, speaking of the three persons of the Godhead living within one another in perichoretic union, eternally pouring their lives of Love into one another. The Trinity exists not as three persons with some mysterious power holding them together, but as an essential whole, intermingling within one another as an eternal harmonic community.

Such a view of Trinity as divine community flies in the face of our Western view of personhood, divine or human, that tends to emphasize private individuality, and the merits of being a solitary saint. The Enlightenment, with its incessant emphasis on the individual, has done us all a grave disservice. In contrast, God is a Trinity in harmony, a divine relational dynamism of pure Love. Trinity as divine community is an ideal model of what Church should and can be, one day to be fulfilled in the reconciliation of all things (Col. 1:15–23).

However, for us to experience some of this reconciliation more fully now, requires growing in Christ-likeness. So this second book in the series is a type of blueprint of what we can do to be more like Christ. It is not about theory or the theology (only), or any one psychological model of what Christ-likeness might (some day) look like for us. Instead, it is what we can do *now* in a very practical way.

For contemporary society, positive change is at the heart of the journey toward personal maturity. Postmodernity promotes cultures of personal dynamic change.[6] Yet, somewhat problematically, within the modern Western Church there is a deep resistance to new ideas and the positive change they may bring with them.[7] Moving against this resistance to change, we are suggesting that to become more Christ-like we all need to change in numerous ways. Christ Himself suggested that this change needs to be deep and dramatic, relational as well as personal (Mt. 18:3).

Based on the interrelational communion of the Trinity, and its forming of the Body of Christ, we see that relationship is at the heart of all that God is and does. He is perfected mutuality, the ultimate example of relationship. In this book we will therefore be seeking to outline in a relational context some of the qualities of Christ-likeness, and to show what we must do to achieve it. The type of congregation that is needed for such change to take place will be the subject of the third book of the series, in which ideas of *therapeutic* faith community will be explored. We also take these ideas one step further in our book *Church as a Safe Place.*[8] For instance, we suggest that it is not enough to find a safe place (a church?) but that what matters is that we ourselves change in a range of ways so that we are more safe as people, like Jesus.

Introducing this Book

The book is written in two parts, which interweave with each other throughout. One part is an exploration of Christ-likeness, proposing a new understanding of how to grow in Christ, and be more like Christ, on this journey. In this part of the book we will refer to many other thinkers who have contributed to the idea of Christ-likeness. The other part is a series of character studies that focus on what it means to be Christ-like today. You can read both parts alternately, or skip the character studies and come back to them later for a practical explanation of some aspects of Christ-likeness today.

We begin our exploration of Christ-likeness with a brief summary of Biblical and recent views on this subject. Then in Chapter 3 we look at contemporary Christian and psychological ideas of maturity. This lays an essential foundation for Chapter 4, where we introduce the importance of positive change. We move on, in Chapter 5, to discuss what it really means to be more human and consider how this equates with Christ-likeness. In this chapter we will also be emphasizing relational wholeness, and its importance to our "meeting Jesus." In Chapter 6 we introduce healing and wholeness, suggesting that these are an integral part of Christ-likeness.

Our exploration continues in the second half of the book, with Chapter 7 outlining Christ-likeness as authentic spirituality. Chapter 7 also shows how this spirituality integrates in some ways with ideas in our contemporary world. Chapter 8 identifies some of the obstacles encountered by Christians on the journey to Christ-likeness, especially the problems created when they refuse to embrace change, and the resulting loss in the Church of some of the language of personal positive change. Chapter 9 confronts one of the main reasons why we do not want to pursue this journey of Christ-likeness – the darkness in us. To help us to identify this darkness in ourselves, we introduce a "baggage list" of some of the potential areas of sin in our lives. In Chapter 10, we look at our "spiritual house" and with the help of this illustration discuss what we can do to begin this journey. We also include in this chapter a meditation for you to use as you actively seek to grow in Christ-likeness. After reading this introduction, you may like to go straight to Chapter 10 to get a feel of where we are going. The last chapter concludes by summarizing the idea of "Christ in me," the core of what Christ-likeness is.

Interspersed with these chapters are the character studies, rather like a book within a book. Each of these studies takes a particular theme, such as what it means to be Christ-like within ourselves, or in relationships with others, or with God. If you prefer, you can read them first to get a feel of what we are suggesting it means to be more like Christ. But please note that they are intended to be inspirational. Their purpose is to stir in us a deeper desire to grow into all that we are created to be. They are not intended to discourage you, because you will never attain them! Feel free to use these sections as you wish. They are not a complete list, of course, and will apply to different people in different ways. But if they are thought-provoking for you, and stimulate discussion, they will have served their purpose.

And Finally …

Why do we need to do this journey? The answer is simple. To be fully human, to be Christ-like, one has to be able to love well. This will involve loving oneself, others and God, each a precondition of experiencing Trinity (e.g. Jn. 17:22–24). For love comes before the full indwelling of the Trinity. Most people have to let go of a great deal of baggage and sin before they have the capacity to love in this way. Karl Rahner saw maturity in Christ as the full blossoming of intellectual, emotional and spiritual virtue in our lives, the maturely-developed capacity of one's intellectual, spiritual and emotional self.[9] For the apostle John, Love as it comes from God (1 Jn. 4:7–10, e.g. *selfless Love*) is the key virtue, for you cannot live well if you are not first loving well. Other virtues must follow in our journey toward maturity. But the indwelling of Christ in Love is the essential need for all of us, and the purpose and the goal of a journey into greater Christ-likeness. So let us begin by looking more closely at what we mean by Christ-likeness, and this capacity to love.

Notes

1. This journey is described in S.B. Williams and P.R. Holmes, *Letting God Heal: From emotional illness to wholeness* (Milton Keynes: Authentic Media, 2004).
2. Throughout this book we will be distinguishing between Love (upper case L), as spoken about and experienced from God and love (lower case) as we know it in human relationships.
3. When speaking of the Body of Christ globally we will use the word "Church" (with an upper case "C"), but when describing a local congregation or faith community we will put "church."
4. The book was a slightly abbreviated version of my (Peter's) doctoral thesis.
5. P.R. Holmes, *Trinity in Human Community: Exploring congregational life in the image of the social Trinity* (Milton Keynes: Paternoster, 2006).
6. Some of this can come across as selfism. I (Peter) address this conflict in Holmes, *Trinity*, 54ff.
7. In the Church, we frequently hear debates about things changing, and the chaos and resistance this causes. A good example is the Covenant or Penal Substitution debate begun by Steve Chalke. See R.L. Shelton, *Divine Expectations: Interpreting the atonement for 21st century mission* (Waynesboro, Ga.: Paternoster, 2006) for a view similar to Chalke's.
8. P.R. Holmes and S.B. Williams, *Church as a Safe Place: A handbook. Confronting, resolving and minimizing abuse in the Church* (Milton Keynes: Authentic Media, 2007).
9. K. Rahner, "Mystery" in A. Darlap, et al. (eds.), *Sacramentum Mundi: An encyclopaedia of theology* (London: Burns & Oates, 1978), 133–6, 135.

1

Christ-Likeness?

Much that is written on the subject of Christ-likeness suggests that if we "live" the Christian life we automatically become more like Christ. The challenge is how we do this "living." How should we behave? What habits should we break? What lifestyle should we adopt? Within the Church a range of guidance is offered on prayer and worship, reading Scripture, and issues such as Christian family life. As a result, our already over-burdened lives face additional pressures as we try to please God by our actions, often on the assumption that this is how we become Christ-like. We feel we must strive harder to overcome our little hang-ups that just won't quite go away, while also hoping that the whisper of guilt that we feel from time to time is prompted by a lie from the Enemy, and is not the voice of God.

The truth is that we do not know how it all works or doesn't work. What we do know is that Christ-likeness is something to do with spending more time with God, going to church regularly, having a happy "Christian" family life, doing our bit of evangelism and service … but is it?

A reading of Scripture and the study of Church history offer a different perspective. They show that rather than merely being about changing our behavior and our diary, Christ-likeness is about Christ being formed in us, at the very core of our being. Christ-likeness is about who we become. Knowing Jesus should and can bring deep change to our character, our motivation, our personality, our relationships, our passion and our desires. In fact, there is nothing about us that will be untouched by the transforming presence of the Son of God by the Holy Spirit. When *we* embrace such deep change, everything about us and around us can then change.

Christ-likeness, therefore, is not a passive thing. It is not something that mysteriously happens to us as we think about Christ, spend time around Christians and serve God. Do we really think that if we lived in a garage long enough, we would become like a car? Sadly, after being in the Church for some years, we all find we know those who are very committed to God, saying and doing the right things, but do not seem very Christ-like. Perhaps at times we even feel this applies to us?

Note the front cover of this book. It has been carefully chosen. If we view ourselves as newly-formed dough, the question addressed in this book is: Who does the kneading? Many times we would like to believe that if we could just put the dough in the oven, something magical about that oven would turn the dough into the most delicious bread. It is true, of course, that the oven plays its part, but before the baking there must come the kneading. Is that God's job? Or do we ourselves have a role to play?

Our own view of Christ-likeness is that it is something each of us can consciously choose to pursue and live, both intellectually and emotionally. It doesn't mean adding more pressure to your diary. It doesn't mean getting up an hour earlier to "spend time with God." Whether you are trying to hold down a part-time job while looking after three kids and running a home, or whether you work outside the home fifteen hours a day, this journey into greater Christ-likeness is available to you. We all have free will and the opportunity from God to contribute in a significant way to becoming more like Christ.

This book is intended to help you along this "how-to" path. We will start by looking at the Biblical background of Christ-likeness and the Christian virtues, before exploring the topics of maturity in Christ and discipleship. These are important foundations for the journey we will be describing. You may want to read through the chapter to get an overview, or perhaps read it slowly, pondering key points that feel relevant to you, and meditating on the Biblical passages we refer to. Do whatever seems best for you on your own journey into greater Christ-likeness.

Introducing Christ-Likeness

When looking at Christ-likeness from a Biblical perspective, we find a range of ideas emerging. Scripture suggests that our Christian life begins with confession. Isaiah, for instance, recognized himself as a man of "unclean lips." Isaiah's confession to Yahweh led to his guilt being taken away and his sin being covered (Is. 6:3–7). The same realization came to Peter when he was first called by Christ (Lk. 5:8). It is an essential part of our journey into Christ-likeness that we recognize the things about us that are incompatible with His holiness. We will be returning to this in Chapter 9.

In the Old Testament things that are holy, places that are holy and rites that are holy are all described as "sacred." Even the priests and the Levites are set aside, sacred to Yahweh. Then in the New Testament, as Christ reveals the work of the Holy Spirit to us (Jn. 14 – 17), we learn that it is not only things, places, rites and priests that are holy to the Lord, but also, potentially, each one of us, each human being, can become holy by the Holy Spirit. The New Testament suggests a permanent indwelling of Christ, Christ in each of us (Jn. 14:20–21).

In the New Testament we therefore see a shift from holy things and the individual priest to the idea of a holy people (1 Cor. 6:19; Eph. 5:3, etc.). It is significant to note at this point that the holy indwelling of people was specifically as a group, both in Yahweh's adoption of Israel, and in Christ's forming of the Church. Congregational life and its relationships should be at the core of our journey into Christ-likeness. This "becoming holy" does not seem to be a one-off act but a journey to be undertaken both personally and together as members of the Body of Christ, seen as the Church.

We mention this because much of our life experience has become very individualistic, despite the clear emphasis of Scripture that holiness (and therefore Christ-likeness) occur relationally. Throughout this book we will be suggesting that it is God's intention that other people assist us, acting as the change agent, exposing our need for change, and supporting us in the journey of ever-increasing Christ-likeness. This raises the frightening possibility that other members of the Body of Christ might also contribute to the act of kneading the dough. We will be returning to this theme in Chapter 5.

This journey of Christ-likeness and the process of change that it entails begin once we confess Christ as Lord, either privately or as a group. At this point we all individually become "temples" of God (1 Cor. 3:16; 6:19, etc.). It should be both our personal and our corporate wish to be this holy temple to the Lord. We can choose to become holy *together* because we are all now priests in our own right (1 Pet. 2:5–9). We no longer need to depend on a priest or Christian leader to help make us holy. It becomes our personal, chosen wish and way of life to be holy, while also becoming more holy.

There is a sense in which we are all now holy: having surrendered to the lordship of Christ, we have chosen to set ourselves apart to Him. But there is another sense in which we have to become more holy by a journey that goes deeper into Christ. As we pursue this journey, more of Christ is formed in us. This process of people becoming holy is the process of sanctification, a forming of the Body of Christ. Reid suggests that sanctification is the process of becoming free from sin(s) as we eliminate personal evil dispositions and practices.[1]

Like Reid, we will be suggesting that this "holiness process" is our willfully choosing to banish or abolish from our lives all the unrighteous sensory, addictive and compulsive habits and sin that do not confess or display Christ. But rather than simply emphasizing the importance of changing outer behavior patterns, we will put the focus on the undoing of the roots of the damage at the core of our being, so that we can proactively embrace Christ-likeness from the inside out. Our first step is to choose to begin a journey to be more perfect as our heavenly Father is perfect (Mt. 5:48).

This description of the Christian life as "a journey of sanctification" indicates that Christians are not merely called to be nice people, but to appropriate holiness as a distinctive way of life (e.g. Rom. 12:1–2; Eph. 1:4, etc.). Scripture assumes that this journey continues for the whole of our life. Who knows, it may even continue in the next? This journey also becomes a distinct trademark or evidence of our chosen life in Christ. The first-fruit, noted by Christ Himself, is our love for one another (Mt. 22:39;

Lk. 10:27, etc.). It is a love that those around us notice. It is radical evidence that we are disciples of Christ (Jn. 14:23–24). It is a love that attracts the attention of others, just as people were drawn to Christ (Jn. 13:35). It is Christ in us.

So on a Biblical journey into Christ-likeness, confessing Christ is just the beginning. It must be followed by our committing to a journey on which we learn to live out the example of Christ through the help of Christ by the Holy Spirit. Christ-likeness is a journey of becoming more like Him, and is accomplished through both our willingness and capacity to change in positive ways. It is our choosing a life of seeking out what it is to be more like Christ and to know Him in us. In one sense, the values or virtues that result are timeless. In another sense, they need to be re-interpreted and adopted by every generation. Our greatest gift to others, and also to our children and the next generation, is our own consistent, mature exploration and experience of Christ in us.

Christ as Role Model

While accepting that Christ-likeness is the goal of the Christian life, we may not be clear about what this means for us in our day-to-day living. There are, in fact, various opinions as to what this might involve practically. What would the Body of Christ look like if we all had significant success in pursuing Christ-likeness?

Christ was a single man. He was homeless and without practical commitments and responsibilities. He wandered off for the night whenever He chose and caused offence to religious leaders. He had some education, and was a tradesman, but was set aside by His Father for an itinerant ministry. Does Christ-likeness mean that we become like this? Let us look a little more closely at the implications.

Christ was a man. This presents a challenge for women who want to grow in Christ-likeness. Does having a man as a role model mean that some of a woman's more feminine qualities have to be set aside in an attempt to become more "godly?" Some people might also find in Christ's manhood the subtle message that there is more of the image of God in men than in women, thereby contributing to a second-class feeling that women might pick up and then feel they need to fight against.

Christ was single and single-minded. Does this perhaps contribute to the struggle of many in Christian work who feel that godliness requires that church life and service come before their family? Is it harder for a woman with four young children to be Christ-like than it is for a woman who has no family responsibilities? While resisting stereotypes, most of us would accept that men are generally more goal-oriented, while women tend to give more priority to relationships. Once again, this would suggest that there is more conflict in seeking Christ-likeness for a woman than for a man.

Christ had time on His hands, at least for the final three years of His life. He had time to travel, to serve "full-time," to teach and to preach. Does this mean that those men and women who work with the church and in mission have more opportunity to practice Christ-likeness than, for instance, politicians, teachers or those who work in industry? If we believed this, of course, then our monasteries, convents and churches would be overflowing with applicants! Some writings about Christ-likeness imply time commitments that are unrealistic to those of us who work a 15-hour day (at home or outside the home)!

As a final area of tension, consider the question of education. Christ spent His time with those who were not well read and who had little training. If we are to follow the pattern of Christ's ministry, we need to ask: How can Christ-likeness be made just as accessible to the illiterate Christian struggling with poverty in Rwanda as it is to the well-educated Evangelical in the USA?

We all know, of course, that Christ-likeness does not mean that we all become the same, clones of Christ. Christ in you must mean that you become more of who you were created to be, in God's image. So in this sense, the more Christ-like you become, then the more unique you become, the more distinct, and the more alive. We need to have an understanding of how to grow in Christ-likeness that can apply to rich and poor, male and female, educated and illiterate, healthy and sick. All of us can pursue a journey, one step at a time, into more of Christ in us. It must not be restricted to those who can read the small print.

Christian Virtues

The central theme of Christ's ministry was the Kingdom of God. Our goal therefore should be to become worthy children of God, esteemed citizens of the Kingdom of God. As children of the Kingdom of God we have to relearn Kingdom values, as opposed to those we currently have. These values or virtues are summarized by Christ as our choice and capacity to love both God and our neighbor (Lk. 10:25–28).

By Christian virtues we mean a range of personality traits or qualities characteristic of Christ-likeness. These virtues illustrate the level of maturity that we must reach on the journey of becoming both more fully human and more like Jesus. They are accessible to all of us. In Jungian language, each of us is on a journey of self-actualization, maturing into a rounded personality, well adapted to be who we were created to be. Put another way, we reach a place where we are fully functioning as human beings, good examples of humanness.[2] So what are these Christian virtues?

Simply put, they are us choosing to behave properly. Our chosen outlook on life is to serve, honor and mirror Christ in all that we are and do. The virtues form in us as we begin to seek to live this way. But first we must accept these virtues, and be willing to change our lifestyle to welcome and embrace them. What happens in practice is that we quickly discover there is a whole side to our nature that refuses to submit in this way. Our experience is similar to that of Paul. He knew what he should do but the evil in him stopped him, so he ended up doing the opposite (Rom. 7:19). We expand on this theme in Chapters 8 and 9. For now, let us list some of these Biblical virtues.

In medieval Christian thought there were seven virtues: wisdom, fortitude, temperance, justice, faith, hope and love. But Scripture lists a whole range of others including joy (Rom. 5:2–3, NIV), obedience (1 Pet. 1:2), holiness (1 Pet. 1:15–16), purity (2 Cor. 6:6), tender-heartedness (Eph. 4:32, RSV, NEB), contentment (Phil. 4:11–12), peace (Phil. 4:7), compassion (Col. 3:12), gratitude (1 Thes. 5:18), kindness (2 Cor. 6:6), hospitality (Rom. 12:13), gentleness (1 Tim. 6:11), generosity (2 Cor. 9:11,13), peaceableness (Rom. 12:18), truthfulness (Eph. 4:15,25), humility (Phil. 2:3), fear of God (2 Cor. 5:11), confidence (2 Cor. 5:6,8), meekness (Jas. 1:21, RSV), forgiveness

(Col. 3:13), patience (1 Cor. 13:4), forbearance (Phil. 4:5, RSV), self-control (Gal. 5:23), perseverance (Rom. 5:3–4), and courage (Phil. 1:20).[3]

What all of these virtues say to us is that to be like Christ is a lifelong character-building exercise that also allows us to mature or grow up. Every Christian is called to go on a journey toward greater personal Christ-likeness. It is why we have been created; each of us is to become the person we were created to be. Not to seek to become more like Christ in our life and lifestyle is an act of disobedience. At the risk of sounding heavy, we ask you to consider the choice each of us makes: the choice to live in obedience to our calling in Christ, or to live for ourselves. Of course, it is much easier for us to choose to live for ourselves, Christian or not, though we rarely admit that this is what we have decided.

Christ suggests that the fruit of our lives proves who we really are (Lk. 6:43). Our fruit is either good (e.g. the virtues) or it is bad. We will reproduce either in our lives (Mt. 12:33). Christ gives us the analogy of being a vine that can produce sweet wine if it is properly cared for. This means going through the painful process of being pruned by God (Jn. 15:2). This theme is taken up by Paul (Rom. 7:4–5).

Paul also talks about "the fruit of the Spirit." His list is love, joy, peace, patience, kindness, goodness, faithfulness, gentleness and self-control (Gal. 5:22–23). As you will notice, these are also part of the longer list that we noted earlier. Scripture describes these virtues not just as natural character traits, but also as the fruit of our growing, deepening relationship with the Holy Spirit. The suggestion here is that as we "abide in Christ," consciously living with the will to be like Christ, we both die to our old nature and also begin to bear such fruit naturally (Gal. 5:24–26).

In Summary

In this chapter we have noted the traditional views of Christ-likeness and have said that we need to take responsibility for who we are becoming in Christ, suggesting that we can all do much more than we are doing. Christ-likeness is not a passive process. In a review of the ideas in Scripture, we have indicated some of the qualities that constitute Christ-likeness, and have shown that Christ-likeness manifests as fruit in our lives through the Holy Spirit.

What follows next is an introduction to the qualities we should be looking for if we are to be more Christ-like. Then in the next chapter we will discuss how we find a balance between God's part in our journey, and our own.

Notes

[1] M.A. Reid, "Sanctification" in D.J. Atkinson and D.H. Field (eds.), *New Dictionary of Christian Ethics and Pastoral Theology* (Leicester: Inter-Varsity Press, 1995), 756–7.

[2] R.C. Roberts, "Virtue" in D.J. Atkinson and D.H. Field (eds.), *New Dictionary of Christian Ethics and Pastoral Theology* (Leicester: Inter-Varsity Press, 1995), 881.

[3] Roberts, "Virtue."

Qualities of Christ-Likeness: Introduction

When we set out to write this book, we wanted to ensure that it had a practical application that could be learned by anyone who so wished. In keeping with this aim, Chapters 2 to 10 will be followed by an exploration of some qualities of Christ-likeness. In noting these qualities, we hope they will help you dig deeper into the daily reality of Christ-likeness as it could be lived out in everyday life. These are characteristics we can proactively welcome on our journey.

The journey into Christ-likeness will continue for the rest of our lives. So we must resist the temptation to treat the characteristics as a kind of standard against which we compare ourselves. None of us comes close to living them all! There will always be more room for growth. Instead, it may be helpful to focus on one area, or perhaps even one characteristic, and begin thinking about this. How might this quality grow in my life? What might Christ want to say to me? Are there areas in me that might obstruct its growth? How can they be undone?

In Chapter 10 we describe in some detail what we can all do to let go of areas in our lives that are obstacles to Christ-likeness. We include a meditation to support this undoing part of our journey. The characteristics sections represent the other aspect: who we are becoming, rather than what we need to learn and do. This balance of letting go of the past and welcoming the future is fundamental to a healthy journey toward greater Christ-likeness. (Feel free to turn straight to Chapter 10 if you think this will help you.)

We have resisted the temptation to include direct applications of the characteristics. Each may look quite different in your own life from the way it appears in someone else's. It will be affected by age, culture, character, gifting, experience, training, etc. It is the responsibility of each one of us to explore how these qualities fit into our own life.

The qualities we mention come from a range of different places. The main source, of course, is Scripture itself, where we find the self-revelation of God's character in His words and actions in relationship to His people. In the Bible we learn about God's nature, how He wants to be known to us, and from His revealed character and values, we see how we should conduct ourselves.

We also have in Scripture the evidence of the person and works of Christ. In the Old Testament we see Christ in His pre-incarnate form (e.g. Gen. 1:1; 18:1ff., especially v. 10); Josh. 5:13–15; Is. 52:13 – 53:12, etc.). From these theophanies of Christ there is much that we can learn both about His character and how He wants to be known. But it is in the New Testament that we have the clearest record of Christ. Here we see at a practical level what it means to be "Christ-like." He is the image of God on earth, and as both fully God and fully man He has entered into material human reality. But there is one key difference. He lived life here on earth without sin. This, along with a range of other unique features, gives Christ the authority to be our example.

Alongside Scripture, another key source is our own human experience of Christ and His dealings with us and others. We are all on a journey with Christ, if we wish to be. Each of us has, therefore, a unique view of God. Nothing more effectively equips us to know what Christ-likeness is than to see Him at work in people, saving them and rebuilding their fragmented lives.

There is sense, of course, in which none of us really knows what Christ-likeness is. It is only after we have either begun to experience it, or seen it lived out, that we really start to understand a little more of the uniqueness of Christ. For each of us it will be different. So in this book, on the one hand, we want to avoid any suggestion that we all need to be a clone of Christ, and on the other hand, we want to avoid setting the bar so high that it is unobtainable for mere mortals. We do hope you can find a balance.

Our prayer is that we may all aspire to learn to live some of these qualities. We do not wish to pretend that our outline is comprehensive. It is no more than a sketch of some of the qualities that make us more like Christ, both as men and as women. May Christ help us all in this ongoing journey.

2

Some Thorny Issues

In this chapter we will confront one of the trickiest problems we are likely to come across as Christians: the belief that when we get converted we are "new creatures," and do not have to do anything more ourselves because Christ has already done it all. But we then still have to ask how much we should do. How much in our Christian life should we be responsible for? Where does God's responsibility end and ours begin?

New Creations?

We are looking at the Biblical concept of Christ-likeness. But first we must understand what the Bible says *we* can do, and what has already been done for us by God. We need a Biblical framework that helps us understand what our duties are, and also what God's part is. For although this process is initiated by us as a chosen way of life, albeit at God's prompting, the actual sanctification and anointing are through God Himself (1 Thes. 5:23).

In Philippians chapter 2 we see our need to be imitators of Christ: "In your relationship with one another, have the same attitude of mind Christ Jesus had" (Phil. 2:5). And Paul goes on to say, "... continue to work out your salvation with fear and trembling" (2:12). Later in the book he emphasizes this from his personal life, "... I press on to take hold of that for which Christ Jesus took hold of me" (3:12). Here we note a mature balance in the thinking of Paul as he acknowledges that we are yet to possess what has already fully possessed us – Christ in us – but also that we are expected to participate in and cooperate with what God has already done for us. But how can God already have done it if it has not yet been accomplished?

Here we see a conundrum that lies at the core of the journey of Christ-likeness. If I am already a "new creation" (2 Cor. 5:17) why is there so much emphasis in Scripture on the part I must play? This is a question we all struggle with in our early Christian lives. We expect this "new creation" of us to be different from the old self, but after a honeymoon period, it usually turns out to be much the same. We know Jesus as our Lord and Savior, and we commit to doing everything to know Him better. We try hard to believe we are a new creation, but if we are honest, the evidence before our eyes is often very different. We are not those automatically transformed people we hear about. For some of us it is even the opposite! For instance, I (Susan) found my fear and loneliness didn't just disappear when I became a Christian. After several years I found myself on medication for my depression and anxiety attacks. Something was very wrong. Did it mean I wasn't really a Christian?

When describing the difference between what God has already done and what we still have to do after coming to Christ, it is helpful to use the analogy of a birthday present. God has already given the present – the most amazing and significant gift that we can ever be given – but it is our task to receive it. We must unwrap it, explore it, understand it and practice growing in it. If we don't receive it fully, it will still remain ours, given freely by God, but we will fail to discover its full potential. But once we start unwrapping it, we find it is such a miraculous gift that the more we explore it, the more we realize how much there still is to find.

So, for example, in my (Susan's) Christian life, I had said to God that I wanted to receive His most precious gift of salvation. God gave it freely and abundantly. He had called me by name and I was His. From His perspective, I was a new creation in Christ. But my personal experience of this gift was very different. The damage from my history was so severe that I was unable to receive the gift in the way God intended. My own journey of growing into Christ-likeness was to be a significant struggle, involving repentance and cleansing in many areas of my life.[1]

Finding a Balance

In Philippians, as we have seen, Paul introduces the combination of *our effort* and *God's working* in us, with a command to "... work out your salvation." Here we find a balance between God's work in the Philippian believers, and their intentionality and effort to work out their own salvation. God does not leave us alone to explore the gift He has given. He actively supports and guides our ongoing journey. The divine persons of the Trinity, Father, Son and Holy Spirit, all contribute to our salvation (Jn. 14:15ff.). In their own unique way they offer us themselves, and by doing so help us to begin possessing the person we are becoming because of the gift of salvation we have received.

Such Biblical thinking is essential if we are to understand what we are doing while on this journey. By the finished work of Christ, humanity already has the potential for transformation, in which we all know for ourselves the power revealed in Christ's resurrection. The journey toward Christ-likeness is thus a journey toward a fuller participation in what God has already done for us in Christ. So the transformation of humanity is first of all God's work achieved, and being achieved daily, in Christ.

In this book we are emphasizing the part that we must all play in becoming more like Christ. But we must think in a Biblical Trinitarian context. We repeat, that our effort is only effective because of what God has *already* done and *continues* to do. All our efforts are based on the finished work of Christ, on what He has already done that is now empowered by His Spirit. But without our efforts, much of what He has done would lie undiscovered and unclaimed by us.

All God's work is the work of the whole Trinity. The Father changes us through the two hands of Christ and the Spirit. Christ by His life reshapes our humanity in Himself. The Spirit in turn applies this to our actual lives. It is the work of the Spirit to enable us to participate in this transformed humanity. What we are suggesting is that each person of the Trinity has a unique role to play. From our perspective, the Father gives us our life in His Son Christ, while the Holy Spirit brings out the character of Christ in us. Having created the dough, Father, Son and Holy Spirit all lovingly participate in its kneading.

What this book offers is a guide on how to cooperate with God's ongoing work in us. To help focus this process more effectively, we must all make ourselves available to Him in the ways He needs us to, so He can work in us to bring about lasting, positive, Christ-like change. If we fail to do our part, God's gift is still given. He has still been faithful. But our capacity to enjoy His promises is much more limited. Have you noticed how many of the promises in the Old Testament are conditional? To live in holiness and know His blessing, God's people had to choose life (Deut. 30:15–20), they had to listen to His voice (Ex. 15:26), etc. Relationship with God is a two-way affair. This book focuses on our part of the commitment, our own active involvement in the kneading of the dough.

There are a range of key benefits for those who receive God's gift of Christ-likeness, but we should note three in particular. First, God has already laid out the red carpet for us. He is God, and has given us salvation. Amazing! But, secondly, because we are naturally made in His image, when we are most mature in Christ, we are also most able to live relationally, as He already does. The idea of solitary sainthood is alien to God, who lives permanently as a divine community of three persons. Thirdly, His divine nature is Love, a Love able to transform every one of us, and one aspect of this Love is our increased capacity to love both ourselves and others. As we pursue our journey of Christ-likeness, our experience of salvation relationally in love will therefore also increase.

So How Much Can We Do?

There are many books that recognize Christ-likeness as the goal of the Christian life. Others see it as a spiritual discipline.[2] Popular contemporary classics on Christ-likeness include Price[3] and White.[4] Some Christian authors, however, do not see Christ-likeness as a personal thing, but rather as something corporate, whereby a whole congregation,[5] or a study group[6] can move into more Christ-likeness. Others, like me (Peter), see fasting as a spiritual discipline that can contribute to our maturing in Christ,[7] while yet other writers see contemplation and meditation as key in this process.[8]

These books are clearly, and of necessity, centered on core Biblical teaching. But many who read them feel "let down" when a book ends where the author(s) are just getting practical. We have so often heard the cry, "I know that, now just tell me what to do! Tell me how to do it."

Some books do tell you what to do. They tell you to fast, pray, meditate, love, etc. But many of us find that our efforts are often spasmodic and intermittent. Our partial success can then leave us feeling guilty and condemned. What hope for a single parent with no time, or a company executive under a lot of pressure, if Christlikeness requires adding an extra priority into our lives?

In contrast, what this book will suggest is that while all of these writings are very helpful, their suggestions are only bricks in the wall of becoming more like Christ. We want to present an overview of what the whole wall might look like. We will be suggesting an integrated lifestyle, a long-term journey, with a single specific goal of becoming more like Christ. Each stage of the journey will be slightly different for each of us, fitting into our circumstances and commitments at the time.

What matters is not primarily whether we are able to fast, to serve, to give extra time to reading Scripture, important as these are, but our long-term commitment to be responsive to the change God requires at any step of our journey into greater Christ-likeness. This commitment of our will is something every one of us can make. All of us can continue growing, learning, changing, repenting of our sin, embracing more of Christ. It is not something we give extra time to. It is what we live while we are doing everything else. We are suggesting that our decision to become more like Christ must become a way of life, not merely a series of disconnected acts or disciplines. We will be illustrating what this might look like for a range of areas in our life.

Does such an approach feel too clonish or mechanistic for you? What you need to remember is that we all bring to our journey our own uniqueness. So no two people will be doing the same journey, though we can all benefit from the principles that others have found helpful. This book lists over a hundred such principles in the character studies.

None of us has fully achieved Christ-likeness, except Christ Himself. But that does not remove from any of us the responsibility to try. We are all called to keep moving toward this goal. Christlikeness is a process as well as a destination. It is the ongoing unpacking of the amazing gift of salvation in this life now. It is an increasing redemption of who God created us to be, which brings change to us and therefore to those around us.

Behind what we are suggesting is another, and maybe even more radical suggestion. This is the idea of intentional, willful, personal change. We are saying that Christ-likeness is not some mysterious power that somehow makes us more like Jesus while we are busy doing other things, but instead is something we consciously commit ourselves to doing, something that we build into our lives, so that all the time we are learning to will to be more like Him. The suggestion is that all of our human nature – our minds, bodies, feelings and spirit – should be involved in our journey toward greater Christ-likeness. We are suggesting a journey that involves us holistically, in body–spirit unity.[9] Such an approach, when working with the Holy Spirit, will allow us not only to change, but also to stay changed. For change in us will be from the inside out, not the outside in.

We must all learn for ourselves from Scripture how Christ lived, and as His followers purposely try to mirror His values and aspects of His lifestyle in our own lives. What are the corners that need knocking off? What is least Christ-like in us? What do others find most offensive in us? When we discover that such change does not come naturally to us, that something in our nature seems to resist it, then we instinctively invite God to show us what it is in us that is standing against Him. We also then welcome the help of others in the Body of Christ as we seek to identify and remove the obstacles in us that resist this growing Christ-likeness. We participate in loving others in the same way. Kneading is a shared process, each of us actively being recipient and giver.

By now some Christians may be feeling alarmed. They may accuse us of being "New Age," or "psychological." In one sense, given the number of self-help books on the market, their fears may appear justifiable. But we are now into the age of "how-to" living. We are moving away from the era of abstract theory. The emphasis today is on pragmatism, as people turn back to the timeless idea that what we learn should change us for the better.

For the last few centuries learning has been disassociated from personal change.[10] But in a modest way society is now beginning to restore the link between thinking and changing. Learning how to change for the better, both as a human being and as a Christian, is coming back on to the agenda and being emphasized again – as it was in the Early Church. The difference is that in the Early Church such change was communicated orally, then written down so that increasing numbers could read and learn it. Now we have vast amounts of written information, which we can read intellectually without it ever bringing about this personal change. So we learn about Christ and Christianity but sometimes fail to know Him.

In Summary

It is very important that all of us face up to our responsibilities and refuse to hide behind theology, or use it as an excuse to do nothing in the Christian life. We must not confuse thinking about Christ with acting in ways that make us more like Him. But we must also avoid the idea that we have to do it all and will one day be judged on the minutiae of what we have not achieved. Becoming more like Christ is something that we all have to work out in our own unique ways, avoiding extremes of denial or compulsive fear. Instead, we must seek to find a balance between His role and ours.

Notes

[1] I have written about this journey highlighting the principles I found most helpful. See Williams and Holmes, *Letting God Heal*.
[2] See W. Nee, *Spiritual Authority* (New York: Christian Fellowship Publishers, 1972) and R. Foster, *Richard Foster Omnibus: "Celebration of Discipline", "Money, Sex and Power", "Prayers from the Heart"* (London: Hodder & Stoughton, 1996).
[3] C.W. Price, *Christ For Real: How to grow in God's likeness* (Grand Rapids: Kregel Publications, 1995).
[4] J. White, *Christ likeness* (Colorado: Navpress, 1996).
[5] C.R. Wade, L. Bowman and C. Bowman, *The Jesus Principle: Building churches in the likeness of Christ* (Arlington, Tex.: Clear Stream, 1998).
[6] H. Offner, *Fruit of the Spirit: Growing in the likeness of Christ – A life-builder Bible Study* (Milton Keynes: Scripture Union, 1991).
[7] P.R. Holmes, *Fasting: A Biblical handbook* (forthcoming 2008).

[8] M.V. Dunlop, *Stillness and Strength and Contemplative Meditation* (Guildford: Fellowship of Meditation, 1970).

[9] We will expand on what we mean by this phrase in Chapter 6.

[10] This view is expanded in Chapter 4.

Qualities of Christ-Likeness:
Your View of Yourself

We will start our review of the characteristics of Christ-likeness with a group of qualities about ourselves. A relationship is two way. God is always consistently Himself, but we often bring a much damaged experience of ourselves. Christ invites us to know ourselves so that we might appreciate being fully known by Him. This will represent a different type of challenge for men and women. It is probably true to say that women are generally more self-aware. They are more sensitive, more conscious of their faults and feel more vulnerable. Men, by contrast, are often more at ease with themselves, enjoying their manhood. Both characteristics are important. With more Christ-likeness we will have a capacity for a self-awareness that enriches our lives and therefore the lives of those around us.

Being at ease within yourself

Over the years you have fully explored yourself. You know your heart, your body, your mind, emotion and your spirit. You are knowledgeable in all of these areas of your life. You are at ease within yourself. You know who you are, what you can be and how you should conduct yourself. This ease is not merely an idea, but something that is contagious, and even the envy of others. They want this peace, this ease that you have found in Christ. This is Christ-likeness.

You enjoy being yourself

On your journey into Christ-likeness you will have gone through stages of modeling yourself on others. But you have reached a place where you no longer need these models. You feel you have found your self, the person who God created you to be. You will believe this and have a consistent view of who you are and who you should still be becoming. You know that you are not finished yet; neither has God finished with you. There is more growing to do, more potential to be fulfilled. But you have enough knowledge of who you are in Christ to be able to move ahead with ease. You enjoy being this person God has created, and it shows toward others and the Lord. You like the idea of who He created you to be. This is Christ-likeness.

Loving your body

As part of your journey into greater Christ-likeness you have made peace with your physical body, and know all its quirks and eccentricities. You are able to look after it, knowing its needs and cycles. You enjoy maintaining your health, without it being an obsession.[1] You have made peace with areas of damage in your body, so there is no lasting trauma. You know that loving and caring for your body is a way of loving Christ who gave your body to you. This is Christ-likeness.

Enjoying the distinctives of your own gender

You know that you are a child created in the image of your divine Father and you are at ease with your manhood or womanhood. But as well as making peace with your gender, you have gone further. You enjoy your own unique womanhood or manhood. You are able to excel in being male or female, so that you can be seen to be who you are created to be. You enjoy being the man or woman God created you to be. This is Christ-likeness.

Never falsely humble

You are able to humble yourself but do not seek to put others down. You are able to avoid showing the kind of false humility displayed by the Pharisees (Mk. 2:18; Lk. 11:43; Col. 2:18). You do not make the mistake of showing off your desire to be humble. Your quality of humility is your capacity never to think more highly of yourself that you ought (Phil. 2:3). Humility is what you have learned at the feet of your Master, Christ Jesus. This is Christ-likeness.

A person of dreams without being a daydreamer

You have learned Christ's perspective on your world and circumstances, and now value it, aware that at times it is uncomfortable. You have allowed God to birth dreams in you, allowing you to see who He created you to be, not just who you now are. He gives you dreams for others, for churches and even for nations, some of which you share, while others you are letting grow by your prayer. This is Christ-likeness.

Having self-worth without unrighteous pride

You are able to think well of yourself while not being prideful. You have made mistakes and can speak openly about them. You have left idealism and eternal optimism behind. You know that with Christ you are a son or daughter of the living God, a person Christ thought worth dying for. You know the sin you would revert to if you didn't choose Christ daily. You have learned that without Him you are nothing, but with Him you have a significant life, and are unique. You are learning to have righteous pride in Christ. This is Christ-likeness.

You do not promote yourself

You are able to affirm the success of others, rather than feeling threatened by it. In all aspects of your life and ministry you have the mindset that seeks the good of others, whoever they are, friend or enemy. You do not need to promote yourself or seek approval but yet can receive praise and honor when it is freely given. Your hope is that by your service toward others they will grow into greater gifting than you have, for the glory of God. This is Christ-likeness.

The fruitfulness in your life

For many years you have said: Let the fruit speak for itself. But as the fruit comes, so you have also seen the weeds, and both entangle each other. You know that one day there will be a harvest of fruit, and you have made peace that God keeps from you how much fruit there will be as you press on with all that there is to be done. In the battle all you can often see is the Enemy's attack. But occasionally you see a little of how the Lord might be using you. You know that the richness of the harvest is God's, for He is the Lord of the harvest. Part of your commitment to Him is being willing not to know the fruit. It is His harvest, and you are happy to be merely a vine. This is Christ-likeness.

A lifetime journey of positive personal change

You value the ongoing journey of change and deepening Christ-likeness emanating from the core of your being and flowing into every area of your life. You are constantly growing into more than you already are. You are becoming more a mirror of who Christ is, and from your perspective this positive personal change will never end. It is a part of your daily life, something you can consistently rely on. You will always have a need to grow and change. This is Christ-likeness.

Note

1 This comment is expanded in my (Peter's) book on fasting (see Bibliography).

3

The Challenge:
Defining Christian Maturity

In this chapter we continue to lay the foundation for a journey of Christ-likeness by making the suggestion that Christian maturity is Christ-likeness. Some may struggle with such an idea since we all eventually "mature," but maturity in years does not necessarily bring maturity in Christ-likeness. Maturity in Christ is distinct from any other form of maturity. The journey of Christ-likeness is a journey into greater maturity in Christ: a journey that all followers of Christ will walk.

We want to look at this idea in three ways. The first is from the perspective of Scripture, noting the Biblical teaching on maturity in Christ. Then we will look at maturity from a contemporary psychological perspective, and finally see how it is understood today in Christian thinking. These are ideas that we will return to throughout the book, but it is helpful to introduce them at this early stage.

Maturity in Christ in Scripture

It is interesting that although Scripture says a great deal about the evidence of maturity in a Christian's life, it has few definitions of maturity. Larry Crabb even suggests that Paul and John both taught that no one can see exactly what true maturity looks like (1 Cor. 13:12; 1 Jn. 3:2–3).[1] One of the few passages to offer a definitive statement can be found in Hebrews. Here maturity is described as the ability to discern what is good and positive, and what is dark and unhelpful: "Anyone who lives on milk, being still an infant, is not acquainted with the teaching about righteousness. But solid food is for the mature, who by constant use have trained themselves to distinguish good from evil" (Heb. 5:13–14).

According to Hebrews 5, all of us need to *practice, train ourselves to know* and *seek to distinguish* whether what we observe before our eyes is the work of good or evil. We might assume that it would be easy to tell the difference, but clearly the author of Hebrews thinks otherwise. He is talking about a precarious learning journey. The passage suggests that any mature Christian should possess the abilities needed to know the difference between what is good, and therefore from God, and what is evil; and that growing up in Christ should give us the training we need. But clearly these skills are rare today. This passage in Hebrews suggests that when we are mature in Christ, we will be at ease in both the spiritual and material realities, able to discern what is of God in both, and equipped to tell the difference between righteous and unrighteous activity in our own lives and in the lives of others. This definition sets a very high practical standard.

Such a definition of maturity is disturbingly practical and experimental. The implication is that we will all make mistakes as we grow in and learn these skills. So what has the Church done with this faith–maturity idea that emphasizes love and requires such discernment? It is interesting to see how culturally bound we are as we apply such passages. For instance, in a contemporary charismatic meeting someone seen thrashing around on the floor in anguish and trauma would typically be seen as demonically distressed. In the time of Wesley, however, maybe with its more enlightened view of God as sometimes being the giver of sickness (Deut. 28:61; Acts 5:5ff.; 9:8; 1 Cor. 11:27ff., etc.), the person would be seen to be experiencing the deep anguish of sin.[2] How would you tell the difference? Later in the book we will be suggesting that it is by being able and willing to differentiate between good and evil in our own lives that we can make progress on this journey of Christ-like maturity.

Why does Scripture have few clear definitions of maturity in Christ? We can only guess. Perhaps it is because Christian maturity should never be expressed in terms of a formula or fixed standard that we must all achieve? Or is it because Christian maturity is always available in every culture, to both men and women, regardless of age and background? The absence of a clear definition in Scripture means we are prevented from resorting to stereotypes. Instead, maturity is about a relationship with God, and Christ being formed in us. It is a journey, a moving target, rather than a simple, replicable product. Christ in us, however, will inevitably give us the discernment to distinguish between good and evil.

So, as a first step, we are noting that in Scripture, rather than being seen in terms of definitions, maturity is focused around a person, Christ Himself. What little is said, however, suggests a competence in both material and spiritual realities, and the ability to discern what is of the Lord and what is not.

Maturity in Contemporary Psychology

In both Christian teaching and in contemporary psychology, we find the idea of maturing and journeying. From the time of Freud onwards, psychology has always seen therapeutic change as a journey, one way or another. Freud's *Theory of the Unconscious* stressed the hidden id, and the need to know oneself by passing through stages of psychosocial development.[3] Jung, likewise, saw everyone pushing toward more complex stages of development or individuation,[4] while Erikson, in the field of developmental or ego psychology, also envisaged everyone moving through stages.[5]

The concept of stages of development is often associated with the word "maturity," with classics from Erikson,[6] Allport,[7] Piaget,[8] Conger,[9] and Gilligan,[10] among others, all making this point. As Benner and Ellens have noted, we are historical creatures, and can only begin to understand our human condition when we view it through a developmental or journey perspective.[11] What all of these models have in common is a longitudinal approach, in most cases moving from birth through to death, rather than beginning at conversion, as in a Christian perspective. Most thinkers in modern psychology see a complete lifecycle based on the process of maturing through growing up or getting older.

So when we take the teaching of contemporary psychology, particularly of its self-help movement, and compare it with the

Christianity's idea of a journey into Christ within the Church, we see very little correlation. Most of those working in the area of therapy would not relate directly to the Christian journey. That being said, a psychological approach can make a contribution to certain aspects of the journey into Christ-likeness. For instance, in order to help someone better understand themselves and their maturity needs, we find ourselves on occasions recommending books written by those outside the Church. As an example, when talking about healing emotion, books by Janov[12] and Goleman[13] are very helpful.[14] For the idea of deep personal change, we may suggest Quinn,[15] while for understanding body language, a very good introduction is Pease.[16] The benefits are particularly noticeable where psychology has moved on but the Church has not.

Some Christian writers, such as Scott Peck, have sought to blend both the idea of a Christian walk with a stage model,[17] in Scott Peck's case based on the thinking of Fowler.[18] In a similar way, outside the Church a great deal continues to be published on the borderlands of psychology, spirituality and comparative religions, combining faith and maturity from a psychological perspective.[19] Benson, Donahue and Erickson, seeking to bring some of these ideas together, have proposed a type of meta-analysis of what faith maturity is, noting its complexity and diversity, while themselves proposing a "faith maturity scale" that could be used as the basis of further research.[20]

Behind much of the thinking of psychology, however, is the idea that as we grow older, we also grow wiser and more mature. Such an assumption can be questioned, especially when we are referring to maturity in Christ, which is very different from other forms of maturity. So although maturity is a big subject in modern psychology and its therapies, not all that psychologists say is helpful for a journey toward greater Christ-likeness. In some cases, modern psychology can make a contribution, but much of the time it has foundations and assumptions that do not correlate with Christian teaching. For these reasons, traditional developmental models have only a limited use to the Christian seeking Christ-likeness, at best occasionally contributing a brick or two to our Christ-likeness wall.

Contemporary Christian Maturity

What becomes evident in reading the literature of psychology
and Christian maturity is the differing meanings of terms like
"maturity," "wholeness" and "faith," as well as the diverse ways
in which these words are used. Little consistency seems to exist. A
traditional Christian definition that combines Christ-likeness and
maturity is J. Oswald Sanders:

> We are as mature as we are like Christ, and no more. He was the only
> fully mature man. His character was complete, well-balanced and
> perfectly integrated. All His qualities and capacities were perfectly
> attuned to the will of the Father, and this is the model, the standard
> God has set for us.[21]

From a slightly different perspective, Schippers noted that the
Greek word *teleiow*, "I complete," can suggest perfection, but is
used more typically by Paul to describe one's objects or goals
(2 Cor. 12:9). Paul links it with completing one's course (2 Tim. 4:7)
or being a mature adult (e.g. 1 Cor. 2:6; 14:20; Phil. 3:15, etc.).[22]

There are many authors within Christianity who have tackled
the subjects of maturity and Christ-likeness.[23] Some deal with the
various problems standing in the path of such maturing. Most,
like Sanders, are extremely good at defining some aspects of the
outcome, what should *eventually* happen. But very few describe the
actual steps you should take. They do not tell you how to achieve
such "maturity" in a practical way. Christians seem to excel in
teaching the need for greater maturity, but will often fail in the
hands-on, step-by-step process that leads to this positive change.
This can have crippling consequences for many Christians hungry
to grow more in Christ. We are taught about God's expectations
of maturity and Christ-likeness, but are not given the tools to
achieve it in a way that can be realistically integrated with the
commitments and responsibilities of daily living. This leads to one
of two responses.

We may admit to ourselves that we are failing to meet God's
expectations and then struggle (often secretly) with feelings of
self-condemnation and guilt. Or we may focus exclusively on
those parts of our lives where we feel we are achieving a measure

of success in Christ-likeness, and then live in denial about the damage we are still carrying. Neither response is compatible with the description of Christian maturity in Hebrews. Neither equips us to continue growing in our capacity to discern both good and evil. The inevitable outcome is despair, burn-out or feelings of worthlessness, perhaps hidden under a veneer of self-deceit.

It is the "self-help" books, often outside the Church, that come closest to a clinical step-by-step model of what we need to do to change positively on a journey to maturity. Over the last twenty to thirty years a cascade of titles has addressed such diverse issues as rape, abortion and forgiveness, as well as emotional, verbal, physical, sexual and spiritual abuse. But none of these books seems to draw the two worlds of healing and maturity together. For instance, very little literature on the development of faith suggests that dealing with emotional damage in our lives is an essential part of Christian discipleship. The impression is created that you can seek maturity in Christ by this "more spiritual process" of faith, while leaving whole areas of your emotional life and history untouched. Let us give you an example of how problematic this is.

A young male teenager was sexually abused by an elderly man and as a result was unable to trust old men or father figures. Some time later, when the young man was in his mid-twenties and serving the Lord on the mission field, God suggested to him that he should deal with this issue because it was getting in His way. In dealing with the problem emotionally, the young man began trusting Father God. The emotional damage from his history had been directly standing in the way of his journey into Christ-likeness, affecting numerous areas of his relationship with God and others, yet there are few books that would have encouraged this young man to see his therapeutic wholeness journey as an integral part of the growing maturity into Christ that he was seeking.

Although much has been and is being written on faith maturity, there seem to be few helpful tools within the Church that seek to define maturity in terms of both emotional maturing and spiritual maturing. On the one hand, we have a range of books that help us on our "healing" journey, while in the other hand, we have books that teach us that we must be more Christ-like on our "spiritual" journey. Very few bring these two worlds together as one personal positive change journey. What is needed is a "clinical" approach to Christ-likeness – a way of tackling the problems in our life. We are suggesting that any journey toward greater Christ-likeness also needs to be "therapeutic" in the sense that it brings personal positive change to our lives. The goal of such a journey should be seen as lifelong, with a clearly identified contribution from us that enables us to keep on changing in order to receive and discover more of God's gift of salvation to us.

In Summary

In Western Christianity it seems to be assumed that there is someone out there somewhere who does actually know what terms like "Christ-likeness" and "maturity" really mean. It is also assumed that someone out there also knows how this can be achieved. As authors, we have not found it yet. Like us, Larry Crabb questions this assumption:

> As we sort through our ideas about Christian counseling and the Church, as we debate the differences between psychological therapies, spiritual direction, lay counseling, and discipleship, we really should admit that we don't quite know what we're talking about. Neither the goal toward which we're aiming (exactly what does it mean to be whole, or be mature?) nor the process of getting there is clearly understood by anyone.[24]

We began this chapter by looking at what maturity in Christ might mean from Scripture, but noted few actual definitions. What is clear, however, is that Christ is our standard and example. We have looked at maturity in contemporary psychology, but while noting some useful things that Christianity can learn from psychology, we also saw that it does not give us the model or framework we are seeking for maturity in Christ. We considered the two journeys, one a spiritual journey with Christ, with all of its accompanying disciplines, and the other an emotional healing journey in which we let go of a difficult past. We have suggested that any contemporary journey of Christ-likeness must now combine both.

Let us now move on to a review of some of the qualities we might express to others as Christ-likeness, before we begin an exploration of change and discipleship by returning to the Early Church to see how the Fathers of the Church coped with the idea of becoming more like Christ.

Notes

[1] L. Crabb, *The Safest Place on Earth: Where people connect and are forever changed* (Nashville: Word, 1999), 4.

[2] D. Middlemiss, *Interpreting Charismatic Experience* (London: SCM Press, 1996), 169.

[3] S. Freud, *Introductory Lectures on Psychoanalysis*, vols. 15 and 16 (London: Hogarth, 1905/1965).

[4] C.G. Jung, *Modern Man in Search of a Soul* (London: Kegan Paul, Trench, Trubner & Co., 1933/1973).

[5] E.H. Erikson, *Childhood and Society* (New York: W.W. Norton, 1950/1963); E.H. Erikson, *Identity and the Life Cycle* (New York: W.W. Norton, 1959/1980); E.H. Erikson, *Identity: Youth and Crisis* (New York: W.W. Norton, 1968).

[6] E.H. Erikson and J.M. Erikson, *The Life Cycle Completed: A review* (New York: W.W. Norton, 1997).

[7] G.W. Allport, *Pattern and Growth in Personality* (New York: Holt, Rinehart & Winston, 1961).

[8] J. Piaget, *The Language and Thought of the Child* (New York: Harcourt Brace, 1926/1956); J. Piaget, "Piaget's theory" in P.H. Mussen (ed.), *Carmichael's Manual of Child Psychology* (New York: Wiley, 1970); J. Piaget, *The Development of Thought: Equilibration of cognitive structures*, translated by A. Rosin (New York: Viking, 1977).

[9] J.J. Conger, *Adolescence and Youth: Psychological development in a changing world* (New York: Harper & Row, 1973).

[10] C. Gilligan, *In a Different Voice* (Cambridge, Mass.: Harvard University Press, 1982/1993).

[11] D.G. Benner and J.H. Ellens, "Conclusion" in L. Aden, D.G. Benner and J. H. Ellens (eds.), *Christian Perspectives on Human Development* (Grand Rapids: Baker, 1992), 251–4.

[12] A. Janov, *Primal Scream: Primal therapy, the cure for neurosis* (New York: Delta, 1970).

[13] D. Goleman, *Emotional Intelligence* (New York: Bantam Books, 1995); D. Goleman, *The New Leaders: Transforming the art of leadership into the science of results* (London: Little Brown, 2002); D. Goleman, *Social Intelligence: The new science of human relationship* (London: Hutchinson, 2006).

[14] I (Peter) am currently completing a book drawing on Hebrew ideas of human emotion. Tentatively entitled *Feeling is Healing,* its publication date is some time in 2008.

[15] R.E. Quinn, *Deep Change: Discovering the leader within* (San Francisco: Jossey-Bass, 1996).

[16] A. Pease and B. Pease, *The Definitive Book of Body Language* (London: Orion, 2004).

[17] M.S. Peck, *The Different Drum: Community-making and peace* (New York: Simon & Schuster, 1987), 186–208.

[18] J.W. Fowler, *Stages of Faith: The psychology of human development and the quest for meaning* (San Francisco: Harper, 1981)

[19] See, for instance, J.W. Fowler, "Religious institutions 1: Toward a developmental perspective on faith," *Journal of Religious Education* 69 (1974), 2:207–19; L. Aden, "Faith and the developmental cycle," *Journal of Pastoral Psychology* 24 (1976), 3:215–30; L. Aden, et al. (eds.), *Christian Perspectives on Human Development* (Grand Rapids: Baker, 1992); B. Groeschel, *Spiritual Passages: The psychology of spiritual development* (New York: Crossroad Publishing, 1992); J.C. Wilhoit, *Nurture that is Christian: Developmental perspectives on Christian education* (Wheaton, Ill.: Victor Books, 1995); J.W. Fowler, "Pluralism and oneness in religious experience: William James, faith development theory and clinical practice" in E.P. Shafranske (ed.), *Religion and the Clinical Practice of Psychology* (Washington: American Psychological Association, 1996), 165–86; K. Wilber, "Spirituality and developmental lines: Are there stages?" *Journal of Transpersonal Psychology* 31 (1999), 1:1–10, etc. to name but a few.

[20] P.L. Benson, et al., "The faith-maturity scale: Conceptualization, measurement and empirical validation" in M.L. Lynn and D.O. Moberg (eds.), *Research in the Social Scientific Study of Religion,* vol. 5 (Greenwich, Conn.: JAI Press, 1993), 1–26.

[21] J.O. Sanders, *In Pursuit of Maturity* (Eastbourne: Kingsway Publications, 1985), 21–2.

[22] R. Schippers, "Telos" in C. Brown (ed.), *The New International Dictionary of New Testament Theology,* vol. 2 (Milton Keynes: Paternoster, 1971), 59–65.

[23] Some are T. Merton, *The Ascent to Truth* (London: Hollis & Carter, 1951); T. Merton, *The New Man* (New York: Farrar, Strauss & Giroux, 1961); T. Merton, *Life and Holiness* (New York: Doubleday/Image Books, 1963/ 1996); J. Philip, *Christian Maturity* (Leicester: Inter-Varsity Press, 1964/ 73); J.E. Adams, *What about Nouthetic Counseling? A question and answer book* (Grand Rapids: Baker, 1977); D.J. Levinson, *The Seasons of a Man's Life* (New York: Ballantine Books, 1978); W. Wiersbe, *Be Mature: How to*

break the mould of spiritual immaturity, and grow up in Christ (Wheaton, Ill.: Victor Books, 1978); B. Bright, *A Handbook for Christian Maturity* (A Compilation of Ten Basic Steps toward Christian Maturity) (Orlando, Fla.: Campus Crusade for Christ, New Life Resources, 1981); B. Haring, *Christian Maturity: Holiness in today's world* (Slough: St Paul Publications, 1983); A. Van Kaam, *Fundamental Formation* (New York: Crossroad, 1983); Fowler, *Stages*; J.W. Fowler, "Theology and psychology in the study of faith development" in S. Kepnes and D. Tracy (eds.), *Concilium: Religion in the eighties* (Edinburgh: T&T Clark, 1982); Sanders, *Pursuit*; T. Keating, *The Spiritual Journey: A guide book with tapes* (Colorado Springs, Colo.: Contemporary Publications, 1987); J.M. Jacobs, *Toward the Fulness of Christ: Pastoral care and Christian maturity* (London: Darton, Longman & Todd, 1988); C.C.L. Kao, *Maturity and the Quest for Spiritual Meaning* (New York: University Press of America, 1988); J.W. Conn, *Spirituality and Personal Maturity* (New York: Integration Books, 1989); P. Young-Eisendrath and M.E. Miller (eds.), *The Psychology of Mature Spirituality: Integrity, wisdom, transcendence* (London: Routledge, 2000); F.A. Thomas, *Spiritual Maturity: Preserving congregational health and balance* (Philadelphia: Fortress Press, 2002), etc.

[24] Crabb, *Place*, 3–4.

Qualities of Christ-Likeness: Your Character and Nature

In this section we are describing some of the qualities of temperament and human nature that allow us to better reflect Christ's ways: the ways Christ would live were He still physically here on earth. Although none of us can replicate these intrinsic qualities as powerfully as He did, we can all learn to be strong in some of these areas, so contributing in Body life to the presence of Christ in our midst: Christ in us, the hope of glory for others (Col. 1:27).

Do some of us have a more Christian personality and temperament than others? For instance, is a melancholic personality more "spiritual" than a choleric one? Is it true, as some suggest, that a spontaneous type of person needs to "calm down" in order to be more sober and more mature (in Christ)? We find all of this a little bizarre, as it suggests that some of us are more naturally Christ-like than others, and that a character blueprint exists somewhere of what maturity in Christ and Christ-likeness should be. If this were true, it would mean that all we need to do is learn and change to be like this blueprint.

Was the quieter, more unassuming John more spiritual than the arrogant, brash Peter? There is nothing in Scripture to suggest that Christ thought so. Instead, what we see with Christ is a range of behavior more akin to several people than one; for instance, anger and tears, bravery and meekness. There is a breadth of character that puts Christ in a league of His own. He had a capacity to confront every situation, every person. Resilience, fortitude, power and majesty were mingled with Love and compassion. He represents the entire gender line for any of us, both male and female.[1] Christ was never bound by typology or stereotypes. He is our example of who we should become, both male and female. He is the embodiment of God on earth. So let us now look at some aspects of His nature, and see how these should work out in our lives.

Consistency

You have learnt by experience and established by reputation a consistency of character and nature that others can depend on. For instance, someone can call you at 3 a.m. and know you will respond as if it were 3 p.m. When you are highly stressed others will still find you mellow and sensitive, as though you are just relaxing. You are able to continue drawing from Christ for others even when struggling with a wave of growth or suffering yourself. This is Christ-likeness.

Reliability and trustworthiness

People know that when you are given a task, you will do it well. When you are trusted with information, with money or the care of people, you will respond with maturity. You have a reputation for reliability – consistency lived out in relationship with others; and for trustworthiness – consistency and reliability built up over many years. This is Christ-likeness.

Being a realist without being a pessimist

Christ knew the very worst about people yet was able to remain optimistic with regard to them. You have begun to experience this capacity yourself, neither siding with others' darkness, nor being unrealistically optimistic. You are able to weep with those who weep, and rejoice with those who rejoice. You are able to be Christ to others, through the good and the bad. You can bring God's perspective in Love, whether by encouragement or discipline, while empathizing with them in such a way that you retain your own integrity. This is Christ-likeness.

You have a gracious humility in all that you do

You are comfortable to be a "behind the scenes" type. You do not crave the limelight. But when needed you are able to share publicly. This is not something that you fear. You appreciate being recognized and honored from time to time, but know that God sees and knows all that you are and give, and that is enough for you. You are known by two: the Enemy and Christ. What more does one need? This is Christ-likeness.

Valuing the uniqueness of gender

I (Peter) produced a little drawing that we have used for many years. This diagram describes, from a gender perspective, what it means to grow in Christ. We call it the gender continuum.

Woman		Man	
Very female	Female male	Male with female	Very male

The horizontal line represents both male and female. This is bisected vertically at the centre, with one side depicting male, the other female. Everyone can be represented somewhere on the horizontal line. All men will be on the male side of the line, although some may be closer to the "female" end in their God-given skills and preferences.

Likewise, all women will be on the female side of the line, although some may be closer to the "male" in their God-given skills and preferences. We suggest to people that we all begin at one point on the line, perhaps moving to a slightly different emphasis as we mature.

I (Susan) have developed a questionnaire that we use to help people find where they are on the line at any one time. But as each of us matures in Christ, we have the capacity to spread along the breadth of either the male or female part of the line. Because the whole of the line is in God's image, Christ-likeness is along the whole line.

Therefore in your own Christ-likeness, as a man, you have developed both greater tenderness, and also the authoritative characteristics of manhood. As a woman, you have grown the sensitivity of femininity together with a righteous discernment and clarity of focus.

Disciplined in mind and body

You have committed yourself to living a healthy emotional and intellectual life, and have made numerous changes to accommodate this. You have a capacity for self-discipline to help you in focusing on what is important to you and the Lord. You have a clear goal for this stage of your life, and an ability to know what is strategic and what peripheral. You feed your mind and your body with what is healthful, practicing integrity with both men and women. This is Christ-likeness.

Adaptability

You can see that your life in Christ has gone through seasons, each requiring different gifts, natural and spiritual. You are able to adapt and no longer need familiar routines and ministries. You no longer set your

mind on a single lifetime goal. You are able to respond
to new challenges and circumstances as Christ lays them
before you. This is Christ-likeness.

Approachability

You have begun to live with the 24/7 approachability of
Christ. While you appreciate private space, you do not
need it. You do not need a world that has high walls, with
a safety zone around it. You do not need to prevent people
coming close to you, or to limit who can. Although Christ
had private space to be alone with His Father, the overall
pattern of His life was that He was on call for everyone
whenever they needed Him. This is Christ-likeness.

Able to think in decades, not days

Your life is no longer reduced to a diary-by-the-day. You
have met the God who thinks in decades, even eternity.
You know He has planned the restoration of all things.
He has redeemed it all already in His world of immanent-
permanent-present. So you are growing in your capacity
to combine God's eternal view with your own day-to-day
practicalities. You value Christ stepping in, leading you
to focus on the horizon, the bigger picture, rather than
the immediate demands. This is Christ-likeness.

You do not need to be in control

You know what it is to have lost control of your life,
whether through illness, a mistake, others' intervention,
etc. You have discovered that you do not need to strive
to stay in control. You can let go, have a light touch, in
a way that allows God the space to do things. At times

you work like a steam train, then at other times you rest, letting the Lord be God. You have learned the difference. You have learned what it means to let go, and have peace, even in the heat of the battle. When the voice above you says, "Let go, I'll catch you," you do not fear. This is Christ-likeness.

Able to say sorry

You are able to admit that you are wrong, that you do not know the answer or that you have made mistakes. You can say sorry in these situations. You are also able to say sorry when someone unjustly accuses you, without needing to defend yourself. You can say sorry that they are feeling hurt, sorry that the relationship has broken down, and you are open to learning from them what would have been more helpful. You know what it is for people to receive your "sorry." You have also experienced bad reactions from some. You no longer need to believe you are messianic. You know your strengths and weaknesses. This is Christ-likeness.

Note

[1] For an explanation of what we mean by the gender line, see Holmes, *Trinity*, 175–6.

4

Change and Christ-Likeness

We have begun to identify the need for a Christ-like journey that embraces spiritual disciplines and a therapeutic change dimension. These two journeys should combine in a step-by-step manner, be available for all, and lead to greater maturity in Christ. We have also considered the ideas of Christ-likeness and maturity. Now we must take a step back and look at the history of the Church's teaching about personal change.

The Early Church and Personal Change

It should be no surprise that personal positive change was clearly foundational to Christ's ministry, and to life in the Early Church. Jesus' practice was His message.[1] His healing ministry demonstrated His heredity as God, while illustrating His values. This ministry comprised, first, His miracles and, second, alongside them, His "disciplining" work in the life of His followers. The first was instant, no doubt followed by a period of rehabilitation that is rarely recorded in the Gospels; the second was ongoing, during the course of which it seems, from the record of Scripture, that all the disciples either showed signs of growing up (getting more whole) or decided to leave Him. The change as a result of this second ministry was just as miraculous and life-transforming as that during the first, though less dramatic in nature. Whether or not we experience instantaneous miracles, all of us as followers of Christ can know the benefit of this second form of healing.

The defining issue in the healing/wholeness of the disciples appears to have been their willingness to learn and then to let this learning change them on Christ's terms. He required significant change from all of them, expecting them even to become like little children (Mt. 18:3). Christ healed people, giving them spiritual restoration by teaching them how to follow His values, while also drawing them into Himself. Skarsaune comments: "Like the prophets of old, Jeremiah in particular (Jer. 7:26), Jesus seems to have thought that Israel misused the sacrifices in the temple to make them a substitute for this inner repentance and purification."[2] His example and ministry brought a call to a new life of holiness, made possible because of His coming and lifestyle.

The clear message from Christ's teaching, His leadership and His example was that all who followed Him were unfinished, incomplete, having a lifetime of learning ahead of them. He assumed that they all needed ongoing personal positive change in order to be more useful to Him and His Kingdom. It is this "hidden" journey toward healing/wholeness that we will now focus on.

Paul, taking up the themes of Christ the disciple-maker, speaks of maturity in terms of union with Christ (Col. 1:28; Rom. 8:29). He also refers to moral stature (Eph. 4:13, *Williams New Testament*). This therefore begs the question: Is the Church to assume that Christ-likeness, making disciples, union with Christ and moral stature, when practiced, should lead to what is often described as spiritual maturity? We believe they should; furthermore, we believe that this is the "healing" envisaged by Yahweh when He adopted Israel (Ex. 15:26).[3]

Life in the Early Church was all about powerful positive change. As T.M. Finn says: "Catechesis was only half the battle, and "battle" is the correct word: The purpose of the catechumenate [the new convert's journey] was literally to 'reform' the candidate ... Thus, as the catechumens' convictions changed from old values to new, their conduct had also to change from old ways to new."[4] Here we see the significant degree of change expected from the new believer (the catechumen), and also the role of others in the church in precipitating this change. At no time does this change appear to be optional, or only applicable to those in desperate sickness or need. Rather, during the first three centuries after Christ's resurrection, this expectation, at both a personal and group level, was a pattern of discipleship foundational for everyone who wanted to follow Christ.

The Early Church developed whole programs intended to "perfect" new converts. By "convert" within a Christian context, we are describing a person who changes their belief and lifestyle by accepting the reality and supreme power of God in Christ, and is determined to obey and follow Him.[5] For an outsider's perspective, see MacMullen,[6] and for an insider's, see Field.[7] Both books illustrate the stringent demands for change made upon new converts, which Field suggested meant a minimum of three years of "training and exorcisms" before baptism into the Christian community.

The radical nature of the change from a non-Christian to a Christian culture cannot be over-emphasized.[8] It was clearly, however, attractive to many, and largely successful, as we see from the numerical growth in the Early Church, and the boldness in martyrdom. The discipleship journey for these candidates was inevitably "therapeutic" in the sense of bringing about positive change by separating a person from their past life. This change would have been dramatic for both Jew and pagan.[9]

What becomes apparent in looking at the Early Church is the simple fact that a process of personal change was essential. All areas of life were under review, and the process was fundamental to the converts' ability to mature in Christ. The kneading they underwent was intended to strengthen the ties between them. But it also gave them common purpose in Christ, and, as they matured, a capacity to carry and disciple others. All of these were aspects of the salvation they were receiving. All contributed to the Christ-like holiness that was to be an integral part of their daily lives.

The Importance of a Felt Faith

Since the period of the Early Church there has been an ebb and flow in the emphasis on personal change. When Christianity became the state religion under Constantine in the fourth century, the demands on new converts were diluted. They no longer had to go through the deep change required, and it consequently became too easy to adopt the label and status of a Christian.

Over the following centuries a gradually increasing priority was given to making an intellectual decision for Christ, and correspondingly less importance was attached to *meeting* Jesus emotionally. Our Western form of Christianity, which has been exported all over the world, is the ultimate flowering of this intellectually-based type of faith. Because it is rooted in a book, we all need to be able to read if we are to learn about it: it starts with our understanding. But the loss is much more fundamental. We have moved from a *felt* faith that personally changed the early disciples, to a *fact* faith. Christianity is thought much more than it is felt.

Today many do not find in this thought-type of Christianity the kind of faith they are looking for, so they turn to other religions – religions that place a greater emphasis on the experience of faith. In past centuries people similarly found Christianity too intellectual, but some, instead of abandoning Christ, sought Him more deeply. This seeking gave rise to what is now often described as the "mystic movement," in which there is an engaging of Jesus by the emotions and the spirit.[10] Some in the Church are now calling for a return to this type of mystical Christianity where one finds more of a balance between learning about God and the experiential mystery of personally knowing Him.[11]

If you embark on this journey to become more like Christ as we are describing it, you will not only learn much more about yourself, Christ and others, you will also meet Jesus in a deeper way than you have before. There are, of course, no guarantees, but we assume you will, because throughout this text we will be teaching in such a way that you will need to feel as well as think. So you will become awakened to Christ, as He would like you to be, not just in your brain, but also in your feelings. For instance, we hope you will find your tears for your sin, and your joy in knowing you are truly loved by God. We believe that both our minds and our healed emotions are very important to you and to God.[12]

Rethinking Christian Discipleship

The term "discipleship" usually refers to the student learning from the master how to act and live. So to be a disciple of Christ means to be committed to learning how Christ lived in order to become more like Him. The type of change, therefore, that God intends as part of the journey into Christ-likeness also touches on this key theme of discipleship.

The traditional Christian view of discipleship is that it means "go and make disciples" (Mt. 28:19). But as Willard notes, a disciple is an apprentice of Christ. Disciples are apprenticed to Christ so that by being with Christ they can become like Him.[13] The Evangelical wing of the Church has been particularly good at making converts, but not so good at turning them into disciples who are becoming more like Christ. Yet the command of Christ is to do both, not just excel at one.

The Church needs disciples to make disciples. But what does discipleship actually mean? If you can't quite answer that question, you are not alone. As Collinson has noted: "Most writers assume that their concepts are understood by their readers within the Christian community and immediately launch into describing the life of discipleship, or methods of discipling. Only a few attempt to define disciple."[14] For the sake of this book, we will assume that the term "discipleship" describes a Christ-like journey, undertaken now with others, of growing in intimacy and maturity in Him.

The Church is already facing the challenge of fulfilling the command of Christ to "go and make disciples," to become *Christ-like*, in an age when people are increasingly, politely indifferent to God. Many are today committed to doing a personal therapeutic journey, often including an exploration of their spirituality, but are increasingly bypassing the Church.[15] Becoming Christ-like, and attractive to contemporary people, will also need to include becoming more fully human and emotionally mature.

Like Crabb, we are suggesting that we have very few, if any, definitions or journeying practices of discipleship that combine traditional spiritual disciplines with a therapeutic personal journey. This separation is easily illustrated: read almost any book on the subject of discipleship, and note the absence of any therapeutic aspects. But it is even more apparent when one reads books on the subject of healing in the New Testament, for even here no link is made. There are some exceptions, for instance, Wilkinson, who acknowledges that health is maturity,[16] but he does not go on and make a connection with the need for a therapeutic discipleship model to gain such health or maturity. It is this "hands on," "how to" aspect that seems to be missing in the Church today. As

Christians, we have much to learn from those outside the Church who are seeking personal positive change and a spiritual journey toward personal maturity.

One of the main reasons for suggesting that spiritual journeying and emotional wholeness should be combined is that many of us are trying to do the spiritual journey with Christ while unaware of our own emotional baggage and even our sin. After putting a lot of effort into trying to live the Christian life this way, and failing, we end up in disillusionment, bitterness or even burnout. We must begin to blend the spiritual and therapeutic journeys if we are to live the gift of salvation we have received.

In essence, we need to rethink the whole idea of what Christian discipleship actually is. What does it mean, and how do we do it in the twenty-first century? We need a contemporary view of discipleship that includes traditional ideas of spiritual maturing, with their much-tested spiritual disciplines, and, alongside this, a faith development journey that confronts and resolves the toxic and negative areas of our pasts, which frequently get in the way of the Lord and His purposes in our lives. We have already illustrated how poison from the past can frustrate God's work in people who are or have been emotionally ill,[17] but we are suggesting that everyone needs to do such a therapeutic journey, for to be Christ-like we must embrace both journeys.

Within Protestant traditions we see a long history of change in people as they come to Christ and settle into church life. But once they are seemingly becoming more like other members of their church or denomination, change appears to end. We demand little further from one other. Other Christians seem to believe they undergo some mysterious personal "change" through reading the Bible, attending meetings, talking about spiritual subjects or becoming more pious. They sometimes see it as subliminal change that somehow takes place without their being aware of it, as if the dough did not notice it was being kneaded.

To an extent, this might be true. Change does no doubt take place in this way since the environment we are in always impacts us. Some sacramental practices, such as the Eucharist, may also induce a measure of change. But we must go further, because deep, positive, permanent change rarely occurs without a focused, intentional and sustained effort on our part. Hands must knead the dough, forcing air and change into it. We all need to shed bad practices, such as laziness and addictive habits, while cultivating good ones, such as exercise and responsible eating. This will take much more than mere subliminal change. Rather, it needs *deep* change that is radical, ruggedly practical and, much of the time, very messy.

What we are describing is a wholeness journey combining traditional Christian spirituality with contemporary ideas of therapeutic change as wholeness. We will be returning to this concept in Chapter 6, but from now on will talk in terms of a wholeness Christ-likeness journey.

Change Separated from Learning

Views are divided as to when learning began to be separated from the expectation that a person will change through the process of learning. In the Early Church the Christian virtues, the fruit of the Spirit and spiritual gifts were all expected to become part of a Christian's life. Discipleship was about learning the changes that were required and then consistently applying those changes.

Some say that the division took place in the 1300s, when a fundamental shift in education occurred. Until then, monasteries had been the focus of learning, and intellectual understanding had been intimately linked with growing in the spiritual disciplines. Becoming more mature had been part of one's religious journeying. But then learning moved from the monastery into the newly forming universities. One of the earliest was in Paris where Aquinas, by teaching theology to anyone interested in the subject, was one of those who encouraged the separation of learning from personal change. In order to study theology, you no longer needed to have a vocational call to follow Christ and enter monastic orders. You were able to learn about the Bible without the calling to a discipleship journey in Christ. Change by learning about Christ was no longer mandatory.

Some see the time of the Enlightenment in the late seventeenth and eighteenth centuries as the culprit. With the printing of books, anyone with the funds could read and learn without having to change, allowing infamous lifestyles yet a high level of knowledge! To this one might add the more recent contribution being made by the modern mass media, and especially the internet, which offers the opportunity to learn online in a purely academic way, feeding intellectual understanding and completely separating learning from any need to change. Examples today are health-care professionals who smoke, take street drugs and even medication for recreational purposes. We call such misbehavior "lifestyle disorder." It is unnecessary for us to live in this way, but we do anyway. Such behavior is irrational, but common. People are aware of what they are doing in inviting sickness, but seem willing to live with these risks. In separating knowledge from change, they show that they are unwilling to take responsibility for their actions.

But something deeper is also happening. The disengaging of our intellectual life from our emotional life is also very advanced in all developed societies. We repress, deny and live a lie when we say, "It didn't hurt," "No problem," "I can handle it." Almost every day we are learning more about how our emotional life adversely damages our physical bodies, for instance, by reducing our immune system.[18] When we consistently deny our emotional life, over time, it will turn around and bite us.

This whole field of study and research is called psychophysiology, and there is growing understanding of its implications for all of us. What becomes evident is that we all die before we need to because of the way we live. Even simple things like sleep deprivation, obesity and lack of exercise take years off our life.

In view of the culture in which we are living, it should be no surprise that in our Christian lives many of us have no emphasis on ongoing personal change. Our experience of learning about God has fallen into the same mould as that of other forms of learning. We focus on God in church on a Sunday, in house groups every week, even do quiet times, but then get on with the rest of our lives without reference to Him. In this book we are suggesting a radically different perspective on discipleship. Knowing Christ should mean complete change, an opportunity for a journey of positive personal change, a new lifestyle whereby what we learn impacts every area of our lives. Each of us becomes a genuine new creation because we have met Jesus and are growing in Christ-likeness.

In Summary

As we read the Gospels, we see significant change in all of those around Christ. He required from His disciples a clear break from their pasts (Lk. 9:57–62); they were to leave everything (Lk. 5:11), share poverty and adopt an itinerant way of life (Mt. 8:20). From the evidence in the Gospels, the experience of growing into these values brought a deep positive therapeutic dimension to the disciples' growing up and maturing. By being with Him, they became more like Him while becoming more their unique selves. In Luke 17:19 only one of the ten lepers returned to Christ to thank Him. Christ's reply, suggesting a further stage to his healing, was that he could now rise up and be made whole (Gk *sozo*) since He was willing to acknowledge and give glory to God. In His life and example Jesus offers to the Church today a helpful framework for a contemporary therapeutic discipleship model.

We began this chapter by noting that personal change was integral to any new convert to Christianity, involving felt experience as well as intellectual understanding. We associated this change process with a journey of discipleship. We then looked at how learning today has been separated from personal positive change. In Chapter 5 we will be moving on to the idea that doing a journey toward greater Christ-likeness can also mean becoming more human.

Notes

[1] G. Twelftree, *Jesus the Exorcist: A contribution to the study of the historical Jesus* (Peabody, Mass.: Hendrickson, 1993); J. Wilkinson, *The Bible and Healing: A medical and theological commentary* (Edinburgh: The Handsel Press, 1998).

[2] O. Skarsaune, *In the Shadow of the Temple: Jewish influences on early Christianity* (Downers Grove, Ill.: InterVarsity Press, 2002), 142.

[3] P.R. Holmes, *Becoming More Human: Exploring the interface of spirituality, discipleship and therapeutic faith community* (Milton Keynes: Paternoster, 2005), 89ff.

[4] T.M. Finn, *Early Christian Baptism and the Catechumenate: West and East Syria* (Minneapolis: Liturgical Press, 1992), 5–6; Skarsaune, *Shadow,* 229.

5 R. MacMullen, *Christianizing the Roman Empire (AD 100–400)* (New Haven: Yale University Press, 1984), 5.

6 MacMullen, *Empire,*

7 A. Field, *From Darkness to Light: How one became a Christian in the Early Church* (Ben Lomond, Calif.: Conciliar Press, 1978/1997).

8 Skarsaune draws upon the Epistle of Barnabas to illustrate the extent of the changes that were expected, see Skarsaune, *Shadow,* 350, 363.

9 Skarsaune, *Shadow,* 354, 229.

10 D. Regan, *Experience the Mystery – Pastoral possibilities for Christian mystagogy* (London: Geoffrey Chapman, 1994).

11 E. Underhill, *The Mystics of the Church* (New York: Schocken Books, 1964).

12 One of the books I (Peter) am preparing at the moment, "Feeling is healing", is based on our therapeutic work of many years, and the importance of engaging our emotion in positive ways, as well as our understanding.

13 D. Willard, *Divine Conspiracy* (San Francisco: Harper, 1998), 271ff.

14 S.I. Collinson, *An enquiry into the congruence of discipling as an educational strategy with the objective of Christian faith communities,* PhD thesis (Murdoch University, 1999), 263.

15 See Chapter 7 for an expansion of this idea.

16 Wilkinson, *Bible,* 29.

17 P.R. Holmes and S.B. Williams, *Changed Lives: Extraordinary stories of ordinary people* (Milton Keynes: Authentic Media, 2005).

18 P. Martin, *The Sickening Mind: Brain, behaviour, immunity and disease* (London: Flamingo, 1998).

Qualities of Christ-Likeness: Your Goals and Experience

Christ-likeness grows over time. The more we make it a priority, the more of it we will have. It is therefore very helpful on our journey to be able to identify our goals, and to make them specific and achievable, the subject of regular review. It is men generally who are more able to focus in a single-minded way, to identify goals and achieve them. For many women goals are always at the mercy of relationships, since women often need to be more available in family life. But the experience of each of us is unique. Our capacity to strategize and plan is also tailored to our immediate environment. So it is essential that each of us should take responsibility for teasing out how to apply these qualities of Christ-likeness in our own lives.

You instinctively seek to do everything well

Because of who you are becoming in Christ, you are able to do everything that you set your hand to in an excellent way. Speed or volume of output is no longer your priority. Instead, your focus is on quality, and is far more people-oriented. You see the world differently, with a Christ-centered clarity, and you are selective about what you give your time to, while being sensitive to the needs of others. This is Christ-likeness.

A student of human nature, both men and women

You have become a student of human nature. You love the idea of male and female, and see them together reflecting the image of God. You know the distinctives, and no longer believe that one gender has all the answers, and the other all the problems. You now know that both men and women have valid perspectives, and that neither is more right than the other. You have learned to accommodate the needs of the opposite sex, whether it is in listening to them from their perspectives, or enjoying the banter when they talk together. In your conversation you have learned to accommodate all perspectives, and everyone feels honored by your contribution. This is Christ-likeness.

Seeking to become more male or female

While accepting that maturity in Christ is best represented by the whole gender line, you also take seriously your responsibility to be a good example of either manhood or womanhood. You know that this has been and will continue to be a unique journey for you. You are able to enjoy the company of the same gender, and support them in the variety of ways that they express their manhood or womanhood. You can relate to them, whichever aspect of the gender they are most comfortable with. This is Christ-likeness.

Enjoying the distinctives of the opposite sex

You also know that the way you relate to the opposite gender is very important. You have gone beyond an understanding of the opposite sex into a place where you actually enjoy, as a man, a woman's perspective, or, as a woman, a man's perspective. Enjoying is more than honoring. It is more than intellectual assent. It is more even than understanding neural structures and different priorities. In fact, there are times when you are able to quote what she will think, even though you are a man; or you can anticipate what he will say, even though you are a woman. You delight in the distinctives of being either male or female, taking them into every conversation, every time you think gender, seeking to promote relationality and not division. With you, it is no longer "them and us," but is now always "we." This is Christ-likeness.

Living maturely, both intellectually and emotionally

You have found a good balance between your intellectual life and your emotional life, valuing the unique contributions of each. Intellectually, you have an appetite to learn; you are a lifelong learner, on an intellectual journey with Christ, covering a wide range of areas. Your journey with Christ has taken you into deep waters emotionally. You can hear when your intellect and your emotions are giving you different messages, and you are able to interpret the discrepancy with God's wisdom. You use both in all aspects of your daily life. This is Christ-likeness.

You have known both abundance and deprivation

You have allowed the Lord deep into your life and He has taken you through rich and lean times, perhaps financially, emotionally, spiritually, relationally, etc. You have learned that in whatever state you are in, you can know Christ there with you. You have experienced His abundance in your life as well as His withholding. He loves you and wants to test you. His wisdom in your life sometimes means He needs you to meet Him in a time when you have little or nothing, rather than when you are strong. You have known Christ with you in both of these extreme circumstances. This is Christ-likeness.

Living the difference between judging and discerning

You have discovered the difference between judging and discerning. You do not need to judge but are able to live with the truth that comes from discernment. Your discernment can incorporate new ideas, recognizing the presence of their author, Christ. You enjoy the lateral, unexpected and original, the novel and new. You appreciate that it is from a person's heart that their significance comes, rather than from their intellect. You know that the person is more important than the principle. This is Christ-likeness.

Empowering others

While remaining mindful of Christian values and guidance, you seek to empower the other person. You allow them free reign in their thinking, encouraging them to share who they really are and what they need to explore. Only when appropriate, and at their invitation, do you make any comment at all. You have learned that they already have most of the answers so what you might say is never as important as what they and the Lord discover together. This is Christ-likeness.

Spontaneity in speaking well of others

You have moved on from a place where you have a duty to keep others humble, to a calling to build others up. You have learned that it is the Lord's role, and that of the Holy Spirit, to convict of wrong and guide into what is right. Humbling others is the Lord's and their job, not yours. You have learned that such breaking of the person is sacred ground that only the Lord and the person can move on to. It is never your job. Instead, you take the role of encouraging a person, being positive and affirming, even where you discern they are in arrogance or self-righteousness. You support them in whatever is righteous and good. You do not take on the role of judge, jury or their humbler. Speaking the truth in love affirms them, and does not dismantle them. This is Christ-likeness.

Aware that you are living well, and plan to die well

This was clearly part of the mindset of those in the Early Church and is becoming true of you. While enjoying the privilege of living in this world, you are ready to graduate to the next one. You have developed a love for all God has created, and you are into helping sustain it, but you are also ready to "go to be with the Lord." You do not fear sitting with a person who is dying and supporting them in dying well, hopefully, with Christ. You know that your time is in God's hands and you plan to die well because you have lived well with Christ. This will be Christ-likeness.

5

Christ-Likeness:
Becoming More Human?

What Christ-Likeness Is Not

For many of us, it is easier to begin by noting what Christ-likeness is not. For instance, it is not knowing Christian leaders personally for many years, or even working for them. It is neither knowing the Bible inside out, nor attending all the Christian conferences and workshops on offer. Nor is it doing all the Christian disciplines, such as studying Scripture, fasting, praying through the night and reading piles of Christian books. These may all help, but alone do not form Christ in us.

Christ-likeness is neither exercising spectacular Christian gifts, nor flowing with all manner of prophecies, words and pictures, nor getting the prize for 100 per cent attendance at church meetings. It is not being a leader in your church, or having a degree, Masters or doctorate in the Bible, theology and Church-related subjects. It is not telling God you will do anything for Him, or go anywhere in the world. Nor is it surviving local church life for 20 years, nor having endured the abuse of leaders or other church members for much of your Christian life. But if Christ-likeness is not any of these, how can we possibly be more Christ-like? Is it even attainable?

Every one of us is commanded to be mature (1 Pet. 2:1–2). We are suggesting that this means beginning a journey of owning areas of hidden sin and disorder in our lives, and taking upon ourselves the need to do something about them (Jas. 1:21,25). Gaining greater maturity means allowing the kneading to begin, and even welcoming it when it hurts! This journey process is known from Scripture as *sanctification*, a transforming spirituality (1 Thes.

5:23; Heb. 12:10). McGrath comments, "The New Testament suggests that salvation is inaugurated, but not completed, in this life, but it is clear that a decisive transition is envisaged."[1]

If we adopt the view that change was part of the Early Church discipleship journey, then we will dismiss any suggestion that once we are converted we become mature just by being in the church and "serving the Lord." Such things may be used by the Lord, but in themselves they will not be enough. We may be "new creations" from God's perspective but to integrate the reality of this gift with all we do in our daily lives, to have Christ formed in us, will take a deep commitment from us to learn to change and change through learning. We must become more human.

Christ-Likeness Is Becoming More Human

When speaking of humanness, we usually think of our carnal nature, which we regard as something to be ashamed of. The popular depiction of maturity in Christ is of being increasingly able to curb or suppress our appetites and other expressions of our "humanity." It is assumed that we become more "godly" by repressing our humanness. Holiness is equated with a separation from the "things of the world." Such a view can easily lead to a despising of daily life, and a tendency to compare it unfavorably with the more important "spiritual" disciplines.

Such a perspective inevitably creates a deeply divided view and experience of the Christian life: bathing the baby is thought to be less "holy" than a time of prayer; going to a movie with a friend less godly than attending a church meeting. Reading a book about world history, going for a daily run, having coffee with a friend, all become "secular," with nothing to contribute to the enhancement of Christ-likeness.

We do not hold such a view for one simple reason: Jesus Christ, Son of God, came to earth as a human being. He lived for 33 years, without sin, and yet was fully human. We know from the clear evidence of Scripture that Christ was not ashamed of His humanity, or of the fact that He was fully human. He did not treat His humanity as though it was in conflict with His divine calling. There is nothing to suggest that He taught His disciples to despise their bodies, their appetites, or any other aspect of their humanity. Separating themselves from sin did not mean denying their humanness. We are spiritual beings so everything we do is also a spiritual act.

Human beings are the only creatures on earth that combine spirit and body. While being fully human, we are able to embrace aspects of the image of God. Giving us humanity was God's idea. The responsibilities of daily life, family and friends, stewardship of our created world, the need to eat, sexual relationships – all these are gifts from God. As we live them, as we live out our humanity, we all have the potential to live in the fullest expressions of being human. We believe that one of the failings of contemporary Christianity is that it does not celebrate enough our being human. We do not realize as fully as we ought what it is to be more human. It would be easy to write a book on this subject alone. In such a book, we would begin by emphasizing our need to value all that is human.

We should treasure our personal uniqueness, our spirituality, and our capacity to be. We must all discover more about the reality of relationality, and our power to love and honor others. We must learn how to be better at maintaining relationships with other people. We must also explore more fully the divine aspects of our nature that allow us to worship and love the Lord God. These are just some of the areas we enter as we explore our humanity. This is what it means to become more Christ-like.

Because of the damage in our lives, all of us are less than who we should be. Our wings are clipped by all our history. We limp through life, never realizing that we are no more than who we choose to be. Some of us limp well! We are often quite proud of being the dough that we now are, never realizing that the kneading has barely begun in our lives, and with no idea of how the Lord wants us to be. Others of us, on the other hand, know we are limping. We are ashamed of being dough and assume God is, too.

The reality is that none of us is who we were created to be. None of us has achieved the Christ-like humanity that we are called to, the holiness of living fully in the gift of salvation in every aspect of our daily lives. But as we do this journey, as we grow into greater maturity of human-personhood, something rather astonishing happens. As we all become more Christ-like, paradoxically, we also become more unique.

Christ-Likeness as Personal Uniqueness

Underlying the individualistic "must fit me" culture of the twenty-first century is a belief in the uniqueness of human personhood. People themselves seem to assume quite naturally that they are unique, or original. They may not feel they are worth much, but they are still unique. This is also the case in the Church. Comments Rahner, "God of course wills precisely that each should be a unique individual and this personal uniqueness he not only received at his creation but is free himself to achieve throughout his life."[2]

Connected to this sense of uniqueness is a discontent with one's lot. Many people outside the Church are comfortable these days with admitting the need for personal change, and with committing to a journey to break the cycles and habits that stand in the way of their maturing. Many are also on a search for a personal spirituality; they are seeking meaning, significance, and wholeness of identity. All these are associated with being a unique person.

As in the Church, so in psychology, uniqueness is not a new idea. For instance, it was the subject of the Terry Lectures given in 1954 by Gordon W. Allport and published as *Becoming: Basic considerations for a psychology of personality*. Allport said, "... for it is the knowledge of our own uniqueness that supplies the first, and probably the best, hints for acquiring the knowledge of others."[3] Many people outside the Church are looking for others to help them become more fully their unique selves.

Modern scientific enquiry also supports the view that each of us is unique, offering the evidence of our DNA, our eyes, fingerprints, saliva and our natural and spiritual abilities, to name but a few. Every area of our lives is, in its own way, unique. We all have the basic tools to become both more fully human, and more unique. But this emphasis on uniqueness also lays a huge personal responsibility on Christians. Each of us has a place and a time in the Kingdom of God, and a unique contribution to make. We are not suggesting a tightrope kind of existence where we have to stop every moment just to check we are "in the Lords will," but the incentive of knowing that we all have a place in the Body of Christ that is ours if we want it.

Thinking this way, does, however, present a paradox. We are suggesting that in emphasizing and pursuing our unique personhood, we become more like Christ. As we become more uniquely ourselves, being more unlike anyone else on the face of the earth, we also become more like Jesus. Somehow our own uniqueness, given to us by God, draws out a common strain of Christ-likeness that becomes more evident as we become more whole. How this happens is a mystery. But happen it does.

Particularity of personhood, our uniqueness in Christ, is most fully expressed and then possessed as we become more human. In turn, becoming more fully human, and enjoying our uniqueness in Christ, means we are becoming more Christ-like. This process is described as *imago Dei* in us. The human spirit by the Holy Spirit is the medium, our wish and actual positive change the process, and our maturity in Christ the end goal. Mature uniqueness of human personhood is to be like Christ. The more like Christ we become, the more uniquely human we must become. To be more like Christ, it is not enough for us merely to become more "spiritual."

Behind this way of thinking is the concept of deep personal change – becoming more human – while possessing our uniqueness in Christ. Such a concept is also helpful to us when dialoguing with contemporary society. In highlighting our particularity, we are saying that it is not enough for us to be clones of our leaders. Many images of Christ depict a woman's face with a beard. But Christ-likeness does not require that men deny the rugged maleness of their personhood, or that women dilute their femininity. Instead, the insight of uniqueness as Christ-likeness gives each of us the opportunity of discovering more of the image of God in us – who we were created to be – while enjoying the distinctives of the uniqueness of others. Men will become more male and women more female on this journey.

So it is helpful for us to begin to celebrate diversity and not a mute conformity or sameness in our natures We should rather welcome the eccentric diversity of backgrounds, uniqueness of natural and spiritual gifting, our callings, our interests and our behavior. All of these can enrich faith community. As we each explore these more fully and support others in doing so, together we all give Christ to one another in our own unique ways.

Christ-Likeness as Being Relational

A consideration of uniqueness as Christ-likeness also draws in our concept social Trinity, giving us a relational understanding of personhood.[4] Scripture is clear that the Church, the Body of Christ, is made up of many, who each make a unique contribution to the life of the Body (1 Cor. 12:12ff.). When one member suffers (or is missing) then all suffer. The implication is clear. None of us, in isolation, can achieve our potential in Christ-likeness. We belong to each other, we are part of each other, just as Father, Son and Holy Spirit are one (Jn. 17:1ff.). As we become more human, we will also discover more deeply our very healthy need for others who are likewise growing in their Christ-likeness. For they will bring us more of our Christ-likeness.

Many of us have been taught and trained in a deeply personal and private faith. Salvation, sanctification and holiness are individual, personal, private. Our own times of Scripture reading and prayer are the bedrock of our spiritual life – and are essential. But nowhere does Scripture suggest that these are sufficient to lead us into Christ-likeness. Christ is present when two or three of us are gathered together (Mt. 18:20). We are called to confess our sin to one another, to anoint one another when seeking healing (Jas. 5:16). Possessing more of our Christ-like humanity is a journey we share together because we belong together. God is Love and Love is always shared, is communal. Christ-likeness is Love shared.

Christ-likeness is unapologetically relational. For some of us this is uncomfortable. I (Peter) have written elsewhere about my own struggles with this discovery.[5] We are perhaps willing to allow God's hands, and maybe even our own, to knead us like dough, but which of us wants other people in the Body of Christ to contribute to that kneading?

The persons of the Trinity, and human persons, can all in a certain sense become *perichoretic*, having the capacity to emotionally interpenetrate one another.[6] This can happen in both material and spiritual realities, within numerous Love-centered relationships.

Living this way, relationally, is *truly* Christ-likeness, the way we are designed to live.[7] But in this process of becoming more like Christ, individuals have a responsibility to build authentic community (Rom. 12:4–5; 1 Cor. 12:27; Eph. 4:25, etc.), drawing others into both themselves and into Christ. Each of us will inevitably find parts of our lives that resist this outworking of Love. It is these parts that also resist Christ-likeness.

To be Christ-like, therefore, is to become more fully a person, while also embracing and living the importance of other unique human relationships. But like the divine community of the social Trinity itself, as we relate better to other people, ourselves and the created world, we are also being fulfilled and completed in ourselves. In relationality all things find their greatest significance. Each of us is more when we are together than when apart. It is the quintessence of human personhood to be able to build human relational community.

Combining relational personhood with Christ-likeness fulfils our need to be more human. It also creates a model that gives the Church a strategic advantage in the twenty-first century, for it provides a framework, offering hope to better one's self, and creating a place to dialogue with the contemporary unchurched. We are moving into an age marked by the authority of experience, so the Church could have a unique platform were it to choose to offer such a model of healed personhood, together with a practical, issue-by-issue application of how this unique relational personhood-as-Christ-likeness can be achieved. For, as proven in contemporary spirituality movements, and the proliferation of both real and virtual clubs and societies, people outside the Church want to know both about spirituality and about how to become more fully relationally human.

Social Intelligence

Over the last decade a whole new field of human research has emerged. Called social cognitive neuroscience, or social intelligence, it focuses around the simple idea that we all have social brains. Our brain is not just designed to look after our bodies and give meaning to us being us, but at its core the human brain's architecture is made to do relationship. The implications of this emerging field fully support the Church's re-discovery of social Trinity.[8] Over the next several decades, social neuroscience, which is based on MRI scanning of the brain as it works, will reshape all that we perceive about who we are and what we are becoming. The reason for this is that it puts us and the design of our brain in a social relational context. This means that we can no longer see ourselves as the isolated Cartesian individuals that we have always claimed to be. But in some ways such thinking has come almost too late, for we are moving into an age of "social autism," in which there is an inability to find the skills we need to maintain relationships long term.[9] For instance, in the USA in 2003 single person dwellings became the most common way to live.[10]

What does social intelligence have to do with Christ-likeness? A great deal, because we are social creatures, designed at every level to be relational. For instance, an MRI scan shows that when we see someone weeping, our neural pathways empathically weep inside our head. We are living the experience with the person who is crying.[11] The potential to do relationship well is fundamental to our human nature. This is the way we were created in the beginning, just like our Creator, as part of a community. But social intelligence also suggests to us that we all need to learn how to fulfill this potential, we need to learn how to do our Christ-like journey relationally. Therefore in this book we will be writing with the fundamental assumption in mind that we are made to do this journey *together* and will find it easier if we are willing to do so.

Christ-Likeness as Continually Transformative

We have already noted that we need to change to become Christ-like. But we must not think that we simply need to make a one-off change, after which we have "arrived." We are not talking about a static goal that, once reached, releases us from the need for further change. None of us, in this life, will be without the lure of sin. Christ-likeness therefore requires a continual need to change; it is an ongoing, lifetime journey. For all of us, Christ-likeness is being saved from our selfish selves and being drawn by Christ into full relationship with Him, others, our true selves and creation. It is a daily journey. There is always more to discover and learn, more kneading to submit to.

We progress in our discipleship journey as we allow the Lord to talk to us about all the disorder and sin that stands in the way of both our finding who we really are, and our wholly possessing the person Christ intended we should be. Other people also play an essential part in this process of ongoing transformation. Living in denial is much harder when we hold ourselves accountable in relationships of love. STOP LIVING IN DENIAL ANNA?

However, God does not demand everything from us without any benefit to us. Christ will talk to us about our sin and damage, but He will also talk to us about who we are created to be and who we are therefore becoming. One of the bonuses of our faithfulness in letting Christ be formed in us is that we learn how to live with a spiritual anointing that expresses spiritual gifts in us. For instance:

- During the course of our journey, it is impossible for us to let go of the sin, disorder and baggage in our lives without then seeing its damage in those around us. *This can be the beginning of the spiritual gift of discernment.*

- But as we learn more, seeing both the good and bad that is in us from God's perspective as He talks to us, we will begin to see others in the same way. *This can be the beginning of the spiritual gift of knowledge.*

- As we begin to believe that we have a personal calling and destiny in Christ, we will be able to believe the same for others. *This can be the beginning of the spiritual gift of prophetic anointing.*

- As we let the Lord teach us how to live righteously in our emotional lives, we will be more able to feel the passion of God. *This can be the beginning of a deep compassionate love for people and the created world.*

What Paul suggests is that we can know Christ in such an intimate way that it involves our whole being: our body and spirit (Eph. 1:17–19; 3:19; Phil. 3:10, etc.). This "knowing" is intimate, personal, yet corporate. Paul describes knowing Christ in two ways:

personally, by direct revelation to the individual, and corporately, through spiritual and natural gifting given to the faith community (1 Cor. 12:1ff.). This knowing is such that we stop doubting and are no longer tempted to question the reality of what we know (2 Tim. 1:12). It is a deepening knowing that never ends.

Christ-Likeness Is Christ in Us

God as social Trinity is a relational community. His very nature as God is relational. We do not see three static individuals standing next to each other but a shared nature of Love wanting to pour themselves into one another. God in Christ steps into human existence, seeking to Love us, able to be with us in our place. God is not only transcendent, He becomes immanent to us. On the one hand, we belong to Him, yet on the other hand, we also belong to others, relationally, within the Body of Christ. If our journey with Christ does not build deep relationships, if it does not create a new set of values regarding other people, then it is not authentic. It is not Christ-like. None of us can remain "solitary saints."

But we also know Christ in another way. In Chapter 11 we will be exploring a little further the idea of Christ living in us. In Christ-likeness we become more human, we become more unique, and we also develop a greater capacity to live and to love others through Christ in us. As Christ grows in us, and as we mature as human beings, part of the fruit is the spiritual gifts we receive from Christ through the Holy Spirit. Christ is the author of this journey. He is the initiator every step of the way. He is the goal, and our companion on the path. Through spiritual gifting, the two worlds, the spiritual and the material, are bridged. Christ lives in us, while living in us together.

So let us redefine some aspects of what Christ-likeness could look like for and in us:

- You slowly stop being the center of your world; selfism dies.

- You begin to let go of your emotional toxic past, letting the Lord help you by talking to you about what He sees in you.

- You are no longer afraid of intimacy.
- You begin *knowing* Christ, instead of just learning about Him.
- You begin to Love people with the Love by which you know He Loves you.
- You can let others Love you.
- You begin noticing other people's needs, knowing that with Him you can help them.
- You develop an insatiable desire to learn, especially about people.
- You begin anticipating problems, others' hurts, and know the changes that can be made.
- You find yourself saying sorry, even when it is not your fault.
- You are the last to speak, but always the first to listen.
- You don't need to know why, you can just trust.
- You can keep secrets, you can be trusted.
- You always give 1,000 per cent, even when you feel you do not have the capacity to do so.
- You begin living what you believe, the miracle of Christ in you.

We are describing Christ-likeness as a deep, personal, holistic change. It is our becoming more like Christ as we become more fully human. In this process we are also becoming more whole, more unique, more mature in relationship with ourselves and others.

In Summary

We began this chapter by noting what Christ-likeness is not. We then explored the idea that part of the journey of Christ-likeness is our becoming more human. We also considered Christ-likeness and personal uniqueness, relationality and transformation. All of these ideas are merely aspects of Christ being in us.

In the next chapter we will look at Christ-likeness in terms of our becoming more whole as people – of our being able to do a Christ-like journey that is also therapeutic in nature.

Notes

[1] A.E. McGrath, "Sin and salvation" in D.J. Atkinson and D.H. Field (eds.), *New Dictionary of Christian Ethics and Pastoral Theology* (Leicester: Inter-Varsity Press, 1995), 78–87.

[2] K. Rahner, *Nature and Grace* (London: Sheed & Ward, 1963), 19–20.

[3] G.W. Allport, *Becoming: Basic considerations for a psychology of personality* (New Haven: Yale University Press, 1955), back cover.

[4] Holmes, *Trinity*, 65ff.

[5] Holmes, *Trinity*, 65ff.

[6] For more on the subject of *perichoresis*, see Holmes, *Trinity*, 29ff., 49.

[7] Goleman, *Social Intelligence*.

[8] Holmes, *Trinity*.

[9] Goleman, *Social Intelligence*, 8.

[10] Goleman, *Social Intelligence*, 7.

[11] Goleman, *Social Intelligence*, 43ff.

Qualities of Christ-Likeness: Relationship with God

Developing our relationship with God is the most obvious area of Christ-likeness. How we do it is uniquely our journey, but it is by finding the uniqueness in our own relationship with God, rather than by conforming to the stereotype of those around us. Which will be the biggest challenge to you in this group of qualities?

The social Trinity and us

You have discovered that God is not only transcendent, but is also relational in nature, and He wants a relationship with you. You know you are adopted into Him and have all the capacity you need to be able to live with God now. You have known times when He is closer than a brother and times when He is distant, without reason. But all the time you are aware that He is at the heart of your life, and your capacity to receive His Love and to Love Him is demonstrably growing. You are also increasingly aware that He is always ready to show you the new things that He wants to teach you. This is Christ-likeness.

A consistent intimacy with Christ

You have reached a place in Christ where you can live in the truth of the moment, but without temper tantrums.

You have a mellowness. Your relationship with God is not dependent on circumstances, relationships with others, or on feelings. You know that nothing, even if it is hellish, will break your intimacy with Christ. You have made peace with the ambiguity of only knowing part of God's perspective. You are fixed on Christ, and have the will not to turn away from the most important thing in your life – being in Christ. You know that one day you will stand before God and He will not even have to ask. He will know. "How much of His Son can He see in me?" is all you have been asking for years. This is Christ-likeness.

A sense of destiny

You know that your life is about Him – Him in and through you and others. You know that you and others all have a uniqueness given by God, embellished and matured by personal choices. You know that you are "becoming" who God created you to be and you can easily identify the recent changes in this journey. But this process is a cooperative one. It is God, you and others working together to have Him more formed in you. You are aware that you are able to make a difference to others, to help Christ be more formed in them, too, perhaps on a national scale, or perhaps for just one person. You do not know the outcome but are pleased to make your contribution. You know your journey has and will be full of highs and lows, rough tracks and super highways. This is Christ-likeness.

A commitment to the Great Commission

You want to work toward the return of Christ and to have your life count toward this in some way or another, even if you do not know how. You believe in the Great Commission and know there will be seasons of your life when you are more active and seasons when all you are really doing is walking with Christ. He may exalt you, or He may let you rest in a quiet place for some time. Either way, you continue to say to the Lord, "Make it count, for You and for me." This is Christ-likeness.

A love and involvement with the Body of Christ

You know that being with Christ is always being part of His Body, the Church. You appreciate this belonging and are mature enough not to view your relationship with God as you and Him alone. You have experienced times of being away from Body life, times of being less involved, and times of active responsibility. But you know that long term you will always be in God's family. Every step into Church is your declared wish to be part of Body life. This is Christ-likeness.

Hearing His voice clearly

We all want to be around those who hang around the Lord, to be close to those who have His ear and eye, around those who can give others the word or wisdom from the Lord that they need. What is evident is that there are far fewer such people than we currently need in the Church. They are rare, therefore at a premium. They are sought after. This may not be a good reason to cultivate a capacity to hear the Lord's voice, but it does give others hope. Maturing into greater Christ-likeness will always at some point mean we begin to hear the Lord in a routine way, both for ourselves, others and Him. This is maturity; this is greater Christ-likeness.

A proven love for Scripture

> You love the word of God. It is food to you, fresh air, Love in motion, your guide and capacity to go on. You are able to let Scripture live to you. Every page, every story, every phrase, has at one time or another lived by the Holy Spirit to you. You have meditated, read aloud, perhaps dissected the Greek and the Hebrew. Familiar passages still speak to you as if for the first time. Ideas continue to come with fluid consistency. Being in Scripture is almost as good as being with Him. This is Christ-likeness.

Moderation in all things – except Christ

> You have hobbies and you have time for relaxation. But in everything you do, you know the companionship of Christ. Through it all you are conscious of the one eternal matter of you and Christ. You enjoy all these "things" but do not make an idol of them. You can give them up easily. You have learned a light touch, a way of doing things that allows you to enjoy freely but without possession. You know that what life is really about is Him, not you, or all your activities and relationships. It is not about what you leave behind in this life, but about what you have sent ahead of you into eternity. This is Christ-likeness.

A fear of God, not the Enemy

> You carry a righteous fear of God, aware that He will probably be behind much of the havoc, chaos and disorder you frequently experience, just as Christ sent the disciples into the storm. You no longer assume that the Enemy is to be blamed for the things that do not happen the way you expected. You have learned to ask the Lord first. This is Christ-likeness.

Knowing suffering and attack

> You have made lots of mistakes and know there are many things that you would now do differently. You have made enemies. You have been willing to humble yourself, to say sorry where opportunity offered. You have accepted that some will not accept your sorry. You have known suffering, have been misunderstood, perhaps persecuted. You know this is because of Christ in you, rather than your own mistakes. You know you have come to the Enemy's attention because of who you are, and you have learned to live this way without fear or pride. This is Christ-likeness.

6

Christ-Likeness as Wholeness

As already noted, in its teaching, the Church has separated the "spiritual journey" and the "healing journey." What one does in the "spiritual world" and what one does in terms of finding healing and wholeness in a non-Christian or therapeutic sense are viewed as unrelated. We have seen that these two need to become one journey. Wholeness, that is, a healing journey seeking greater personal authenticity, should be an essential part of our "spiritual" journey of becoming more like Christ. This is not as radical as it may sound. As Christians, we all believe that Christ must possess every area of our lives, that he must be at the very core of our being. He should shape our values, body and outlook. So how has the split even happened? How is it that so many of our positive change values have been hijacked by psychology and all its therapies?

From the late 1800s psychology began to develop as a discipline in its own right. In doing so, it took over a number of ideas and practices that had traditionally been part of Church life and journeying. During the twentieth century in particular, psychology owned, labeled and expanded a range of ideas that had been part of our Christian heritage, as Oden powerfully demonstrates.[1] This upstart pretender to the Christian throne has been so successful that today therapists are the new priests, and many Christians go to them because they cannot find help in the Church, which now only offers "spiritual" help. Yet in the Early Church it was part of church life to give help to the sick, poor and widows (Acts 6:1ff.). Likewise, well before psychology and its therapies began to appear, the Quakers were already building and running the first mental hospital in the world, at The Retreat in York.

So in exploring the connection between Christ-likeness and personal "therapeutic" change, we must accept that much that is now the field of psychology and its therapies was originally part of Christianity and therefore of the journey into maturity in Christ. For instance, it was traditionally assumed that alcoholics who turned to Christ would break their addiction to alcohol, but now they would be expected to go to a therapist. As a Church, we no longer possess the skills needed to treat addiction. Instead, we buy them in from therapeutic practice. Today the Church is not seen as a rescue centre, but a place for nice successful people.

On the positive side, psychology, in taking up traditional Christian ideas, such as the teaching that being more baggage free is being more healthy, has developed them in ways beyond anything the Church envisaged.[2] The sad thing is that Christianity is now only just beginning to realize the good and the bad of psychology, and to understand what we need to learn from it in order to develop a contemporary Christ-like wholeness journey model. One of the biggest challenges for the Church is the question of wholeness. What does it mean to be whole in the twenty-first century? When the dough has been baked, and has become delicious bread, what might it really look like from God's perspective?

Christ-Likeness as Becoming More Whole

Human nature and existence are inexhaustibly complex, which makes any effort at a definition of human wholeness almost impossible.[3] But we can look at how both psychology and Christianity have used the word "wholeness" in the past.

Within psychology, "wholeness" is related to journeying, but one struggles to find consistent references to this term in most psychology textbooks. For instance, the word is absent as a concept or subject in the recent tome published by the American Psychological Association and focusing on the clinical aspects of spirituality.[4] Even the Shorter Oxford English Dictionary does not have a full entry for wholeness, instead, slipping it under the term "whole." Brown (OED) describes wholeness as, "a whole, with respect to the whole."[5] Only on the fringes of psychology, in self-help books, can the word be found.[6] Probably no consistent definition seems to exist because "wholeness" is not a keyword in psychology. When applied to human personhood, it would probably have a core meaning along the lines of "to be complete," or "to be one."

Within Western Christianity, the word fares much better, with numerous book titles using the word "wholeness."[7] It is a word widely adopted by Christian authors. But these same authors seem to use a range of definitions depending on the domain of the book, for instance, personal faith development, relationship with God, building community, recovery from mental and emotional illness, etc. Behind all of these ideas of wholeness are two concepts. One is Hebrew, the other Greek.

Taking the Hebrew perspective, in Genesis chapters 2 and 3 we are introduced to the idea of the existence of material matter, the physical human body with the breath of God flowing into it, so animating it (Gen. 2:7). The suggestion is that "man" was a unique creation in the image of God (*imago Dei*). In our work, we therefore describe human make-up as "body–spirit" unity. When Spirit merges into matter it animates it to human personhood, in the image of God. The Holy Spirit co-inheres in human spirit, offering the potential of Christ-likeness, Christ in us. So human personhood is one united whole, body and spirit, remaining one whole while spirit/Spirit and matter continue to co-mingle within one another (Job 34:14–15). When body and spirit separate, by willful surrender (Mt. 27:50; Acts 7:59) or the onset of death, physical matter "dies," returning to the earth it came from (Gen. 2:7; 18:27; Ps. 90:3, etc.), while the human spirit continues to exist. When body–spirit unity no longer exists, human life on earth as we know it is no longer sustainable. Wholeness, in this sense, is the maturing of body–spirit unity within material reality as we become more like Christ. Hebrew thinking emphasizes the wholeness of human nature embracing spirit and body, rather than its distinct parts.

From its Hebrew roots, the Greek-speaking Early Church held to a similar idea.[8] Human nature is *totus homo*, a total whole. God created the whole person, body and spirit, and Christ came to save the whole person, body and spirit, because the whole person is damaged by sin.[9] If people accept salvation, they will know resurrection of the whole person, body and spirit, and this whole person will stand before God.

We use these two simple perspectives, the Hebrew and Greek, to suggest that in the Old Testament, New Testament and in the Early Church there was a consistency in the understanding of wholeness. Gibson gives a helpful background to these ideas.[10] Taking up this theme, Popkes proposes that the Church must first recognize God as "whole," thereby implying that we also can be whole.[11] God's nature is wholeness. He is whole by being Himself, and we are created to enjoy human wholeness in His image. But the impact of sin, together with our willfulness, has divided us from ourselves, others and God. So for any of us to attain wholeness, the way we were created to enjoy it, a process of growth and change is required, a journey that brings to an end selfism and its fragmentation.

Our Christ-like wholeness should in turn produce in us and out of us a range of positive qualities, including the Christian virtues (e.g. divine Love in human life made manifest) and the fruit and gifts of the Spirit. With this Love also comes a range of other abilities, such as being able to disciple others to help them catch and grow this Love. It also produces a growing ability to hear God's will and ways, discern good and evil and live consistently in likeness to Christ. Beuchner suggests that if we are to enjoy wholeness, we should have a capacity to see all reality from God's perspective,[12] while Goldbrunner defined wholeness as a journey possessing greater holiness.[13] Both are different but helpful ways of talking about wholeness in Christ.

Benner also reminds us that well-being and wholeness are not the hope or goal of the Kingdom. Union with Christ is.[14] While noting his comment, in our work we see wholeness, well-being and capacity for relationality as all essential parts of Christ-likeness. Roger Hurding has done a very competent job of bringing these ideas together within the concept of wholeness as a therapeutic journey.[15]

In a range of areas we are therefore on safe ground in using the term wholeness to describe our journey into greater Christ-likeness. Words like "maturity" and "stage development" are inadequate. But we have one more aspect of Christ-likeness to take on board before we have a definition that we can work with. This is the spiritual aspect of this journey. It is a subject we need to think through carefully before we can more fully incorporate it into our journey model of becoming more like Christ.

"Therapeutic" Change, Christ-Likeness and Discipleship

We have begun to recognize that positive change is essential to our being wholly alive. We are describing this as a wholeness journey of personal transformation facilitated by a God who, through the Holy Spirit, co-inheres in all things in heaven and earth with the power to make all things whole. Becoming whole requires a God-focused, lived reality, and our change, so that Christ-likeness also becomes our lived reality.

In reading Scripture, I (Peter) began to see that transformative change was the common experience of many Biblical personalities. Just look at people like Joseph, Moses, David, and Peter, for instance. All had a difficult path to walk in growing up. Many Christians experience the bringing together of these two distinct ideas: the spiritual discipline of a journey into greater Christ-likeness, and the need for personal positive change. In the "folk psychology" of our contemporary culture, this positive change is more commonly described as "therapeutic."[16] In response, the Church needs to begin to develop ideas of what it means to be Christ-like regarding all the baggage that psychology suggests is fragmenting us and making us ill.

Many in the Church, particularly in the Evangelical tradition, would argue that God has called the Church to the Great Commission and "eternal" questions, not "navel-gazing." Some in the Church are suspicious of such therapeutic introspection, and even alarmed, seeing therapy as dangerous. But what we are noting is that both in the Early Church, and at defining moments of the Church's history, a return to this holistic positive change has revitalized the Church. An outstanding example of the Church finding new meaning and life is John Wesley, with his band and class meetings.[17] With his support, people enjoyed nothing more than the pursuit of spiritual conversation and moral personal growth, "speaking without reserve."[18] These meetings combined the Protestant doctrine of grace and the Catholic ethic of holiness.[19] For evidence of the therapeutic nature of these class meetings, see Henderson.[20] It is interesting that though the beginning of group psychological therapy is normally traced to Dr J.H. Pratt's work with TB patients in 1905,[21] a century and a half before Pratt, Wesley was using the same therapeutic practices.[22]

An integral part of Christian discipleship, therefore, is our need to live as though our toxic pasts never occurred, as though we have seen all the symptoms go, once and for all. But by that we do not mean that we should live in denial, or repress our pain. Instead, we should learn how to give it to Christ, with all its roots and drives. This is something we can all do as part of a journey with Christ and has been described by us in other writings.[23] When they hear us teach this possibility of being free from our past by giving it to Christ, many find it unbelievable. It seems inconceivable that they could be free in this way. Modern biomedicine or psychological therapies cannot offer this. Here the normal pathway is to teach a person how to manage their disorders, not be free from them. Freedom is something only Christ offers.

This "therapeutic" process, as we have been practicing it now for many years, is intended to bring everyone to a point where only the empty memories of their toxic pasts remain. The actual emotional pain has been successfully given to Christ, absorbed into the cross. This wholeness or "therapeutic" journey is our owning and giving to Christ all the stored-up toxic pain of our pasts that hold us back from possessing our futures. It is a therapeutic process in which we let go and give to Christ all the shame and stigma of our lost and stolen years.

But this is only part of the story. We not only allow Christ to take our damaged pasts, we also invite Him to redeem the years in such a way that we recover ground lost because of our damaged sinful pasts, and, with Christ's help, begin to live as though they never occurred. We begin to taste a God-given wholeness that we have never known before, the mouth-watering bread made from dough kneaded by the Master. This has already been the discovery of many.[24] We experience a recreation and redeeming of the person God created us to be.

We are comfortable calling this process journey "therapeutic" because it combines elements more normally described in psychological therapies, while from the spiritual perspective we are becoming more wholly who God created us to be. This is in contrast to our remaining who we now are. So our definition of "therapeutic" is unlike that used in psychology, for it is the message and hope of the gospel of the Kingdom in this life. It is what Christ means when He says we must be "born from above" (Jn. 3:3).[25] This

is redemption with transformation, a healing of the whole person.
This is what we believe the gospel of salvation truly offers.

What Does This Christ-like Journey Now Look Like?

We are suggesting that the promises of Christ are that we can
embrace wholeness now. In this way, we are able to reconcile what
He taught and lived with what needs to happen to every one of
us today. It means that Christ-likeness ceases to be merely a faith
claim that is intellectual but little experienced, and becomes a
life-changing, visible and integrated journey within our daily
relationships and responsibilities.

But to do this journey we will need to look at ourselves in ways
we have not done in the past. For instance, with the help of the Lord,
each of us can undertake what we call "homework," that is, time
spent reflecting and praying about what the Lord tells us He sees
in us. In the course of our homework, we can admit to mistakes
in our pasts, things we have done wrong, and can find cleansing
at an emotional level from loss, pain and our shame. Perhaps we
will discover that we held a view of Scripture or church life that
has not been helpful to us, or maybe we will find an unwillingness
to entertain intellectual enquiry. Perhaps we have been content to
believe what others have taught us, without growing the capacity
to listen to the Lord ourselves. In Chapter 10 we will describe more
of how this journey can be undertaken.

The journey may be described as "our harnessing through
Christ the human capacity for personal positive transformative
change toward Christ-likeness, by owning our sin and letting go
of our toxic pasts." This is a gradual *salugenic* (wholeness giving)
discipleship journey. It takes place within the womb of faith
community where together we possess the fullness of who we
all might become. This is our personal journey, in the course of
which we realize our full creative potential, our *imago Dei*. We
begin by acknowledging that we no longer wish to remain who
we now are.

Christ-likeness, therefore, correlates with realizing our full
potential in Christ within faith community. It is our *becoming* in
Christ who He created us to be by beginning to live a personally

significant life. This is the goal of our life in Christ. But we need to include a caution here. It seems that there is a direct link between the level of need in our lives, and the attractiveness of this journey to us. For instance, the more successful we feel we are as Christians, the less desperate we are for salugenic, wholeness-giving change. If we think we are all right, then we don't feel a need to change. Many in the Church today are in this place of not feeling any need to change.

Likewise, if our theology tells us that our pasts are already dealt with, regardless of the evidence in our personal lives, we will probably be unwilling to see either the sin or our need for change. A "triumphalist" theology will suggest to us that we are already living in the fullness of Christ, so we will not be open to the idea that we need to return to our difficult pasts.

A model like the one we are suggesting will inevitably be more attractive to those who are able to admit that they have not yet achieved the wholeness and intimacy with Christ that they are seeking. It is a particularly relevant message for the sick, the poor, the emotionally ill and the underprivileged, etc. Were not these the people Christ told us to go to (Mt. 10:8; Lk. 9:2, etc.)? We all need in our lives the hope and experience of positive change toward wholeness, but many of us have not been ready to admit this need.

As authors, we hope that describing the journey in this way will help to make your own admission more of a reality. Elsewhere, we have described this as the *Rapha* journey (Holmes 2005: 83ff.).

Taking Personal Responsibility

To begin a wholeness discipleship journey requires a significant shift in the thinking of most Christians. Followers of Christ need to admit that the way they presently are is not good, that they need to change. This comes as a challenge since we live in an age when healing and wholeness have largely become the responsibility of professional others. The perception of most of us is that anything "therapeutic" or related to positive change is done to us by others. Therapists tell us what we need to do in order to get healed.

This mindset is not only found in contemporary culture, but is also prevalent in the Church. For instance, within the Charismatic tradition, people may be encouraged to relax, open their hands *to receive from God* and do nothing more themselves while they are *prayed for by others.* They are not to strive, but to accept passively from the Lord or from those praying.[26] We are merely spectators in our own healing. This can be illustrated from a US healthcare context. Boyd writes: "The mental health movement has turned us into a nation of victims. If we aren't victimized by abusive parents or spouses, we are victims of cognitive impairment, attention deficiency, economic plight, guilt-inducing religion, or subtle discrimination of people like us."[27] Along similar lines, our observation is that some psychological therapies can actually promote feelings of helplessness, victimization and dependency. We all end up, if we can afford it, going to a therapist.

Furedi offers some disturbing additional observations to this thinking from here in the UK. He comments that the subtle persuasive growth of this "health" culture brings with it a passivity where work is seen as stressful, examinations and competition as "child abuse," and all decision-making as a possible health hazard. In both domains, Church and society, others are ultimately responsible for any positive change in us. I am merely the passive receptor. Someone else is paid to do the work for me.[28]

What we are proposing is the need for a radical shift in the mindset of anyone who wishes to learn Christ-likeness as a journey. We all need to stop blaming others (or God) for our damage, sickness or failure to grow as Christians. Instead, we need to make a renewed commitment to be responsible with and for ourselves.

Because the cost of doing this journey requires discipline and will be painful, we need to be "hungry" for positive Christ-like change. Without a tenacious commitment we will quit when it gets tough. The reasons are not difficult to find. Few things on earth are more Kingdom building than men and women moving in spiritual maturity in Christ-likeness. The divine capacity to Love, the ability to be at ease in both realities, the living of spiritual gifting, etc. are all a profound threat to the Enemy. Anything that is important to God – for example, seeing Christ formed in us – will inevitably be of keen interest to the Enemy.

In giving responsibility for our disorders to others, we deny ourselves the opportunity to advance in Christ.[29] Our journeys will only be as successful as they are. If the pastor has a good sermon, we may discover more Christ-likeness that week. But what if the pastor is not having a good day? Taking personal responsibility for ongoing change means that the kneading can continue from the Lord irrespective of other people. Adopting the concept of Christ-likeness being a healing journey, is therefore something we must do *for* ourselves *to* ourselves, and not have others do to or for us. No one, not even God, can ultimately take away from us our personal responsibility for ourselves: our health, well-being, relationships and wholeness. No one else can acquire our wholeness for us (e.g. Jn. 1:12–13; Phil. 2:12–15; 1 Thes. 2:13, etc.). Even Christ cannot take upon Himself all that is ours until we first choose to take upon ourselves all that is ours.

We see this unwillingness to emphasize personal responsibility as one of the great failures of psychological therapies, especially within the human potential movement. The suggestion is that others (therapists) give us healing and wholeness much as the store sells us groceries. Such passivity is one of the diseases of both our society and the Church. Our Western culture, the Church included, is now saturated with the mindset of "the helping professions"[30] and, "Counseling is the appropriate avenue for ameliorating all sorts of disturbances in people's lives."[31]

In contrast, wholeness in Christ is our living well, having found fullness in our selves, with others and with God, because Christ Himself is the only true wholeness any one of us will ever know. Wholeness becomes a matter of right thinking, right feeling and right living, a journey into Christ. But wholeness will never mean being fully complete or perfect. Rather, it means having the capacity to live more fully while living Christ. In God this wholeness can never be diminished for it is founded on Christ, through the help of the social Trinity. Anything less than God Himself cannot be this wholeness, or give us fullness of humanness. But this journey toward Christ-likeness through the medium of salugenic discipleship can only begin as we take responsibility for who we now are. With Christ as our wholeness, we are able to become more fully human and also live a more significant life.

Our View of Christ-Likeness

Over the years I (Peter) have used a whole range of ideas and phrases to describe these combined ideas. We could call this journey therapeutic discipleship, or discipleship as change. But we are also describing discipleship as wholeness, suggesting that all areas of our life have to change if we are to be more like Christ. Enshrined in this concept of Christ-likeness is the idea of continuing therapeutic wholeness change as a journey. Discipleship, wholeness and maturity should thus combine traditional Christ-centered values and spirituality, but also include a therapeutic wholeness. So from now on we will use the terms "disciple(ship)," "journey," "clinical," "salugenic" and "wholeness" in this complete sense, to describe a person who is committed to this journey of discipleship change.

What we are proposing is therefore not just a new knowledge of Christian truth, but a life-changing journey. The way we are most comfortable describing Christ-likeness is that it is a personal positive change journey in a faith community or faith relational setting, leading to the ongoing wholeness of Christ being formed in us.

Does that sound exciting to you? Does it feel like a journey you would want to walk, to take responsibility for? We have the opportunity of sharing in the journey of Christ-likeness walked by many over so many centuries and in so many cultures. Though the kneading of the dough may be painful, we can invite God and others to stand with us. We can see our lives being changed as we discover the freedom from our history that is promised in the gift of salvation. We can find consistency in the spiritual disciplines as they are integrated into our daily lives because the baggage from our pasts no longer opposes it. We can know Christ being formed in us and actively share in the journey of Christ being formed in others.

Notes

1. T.C. Oden, "The historic pastoral care tradition: A resource for Christian psychologists," *Journal of Psychology and Theology* 20 (1992), 2:137–146.
2. A good recent example is the emerging field of social intelligence, or social cognitive neuroscience, to which we have already referred, which emphasizes that our brain is social in design, see Goleman, *Social Intelligence*.
3. J.B. Cobb, *Theology and Pastoral Care* (Philadelphia: Fortress Press, 1977).
4. E.P. Shafranske (ed.), *Religion and the Clinical Practice of Psychology* (Washington: American Psychological Association, 1996).
5. L. Brown, *New Shorter Oxford English Dictionary*, vol. 2 (Oxford: Clarendon Press, 1993). A search on the Psych-Info database for "wholeness" showed 116 articles on wholeness, while 1,440 articles refer to healing and 4,609 to maturity. In a search made in March 2004 on the ISI Web of Science database (incorporating the social sciences, arts, humanities and general sciences), of 33 million items, 472 had "wholeness" in their title, subject or abstract, while 26,599 had "maturity," and 43,449 had "healing."
6. At the Inner Bookshop in Oxford, UK (www.innerbookshop.com), there are 69 books with "wholeness" as the keyword, while 2,044 have healing as the keyword.
7. See, for example, J. Goldbrunner, *Holiness is Wholeness* (London: Burns & Oates, 1955); N. Auten, *From Fear to Faith: Studies of suffering and wholeness* (London: SPCK, 1971); N. Goudie, *Developing Spiritual Wholeness* (London: World Books/Word, 1972/1992); S. Hughes, *God Wants You Whole: The way to healing, health and wholeness* (Eastbourne: Kingsway, 1984); M. Ashton, *Growing in Wholeness* (Eastbourne: Kingsway, 1985); H. Booth, *Healing is Wholeness: A resource book to encourage healing ministry initiatives in the local church* (London: The Churches Council for Health and Healing, 1987); J.E. Adams, *A Thirst for Wholeness: How to gain wisdom from the book of James* (Stanley, N.C.: Timeless Texts 1988/1997); R. Frost, *Christ and Wholeness* (Eastbourne: Kingsway, 2000); A. le Peau, *Ephesians: Wholeness for a broken world* (London: Inter-Varsity Press/SU, 2000); J. Gross, *One: Returning to wholeness* (New York: Tabby House/Portico Press, 2004); Williams and Holmes, *Letting God Heal*; etc.
8. Skarsaune, *Shadow*.
9. A. Nygren, *Agape and Eros* (London: SPCK, 1937, Chicago: Chicago Press, 1982), 339.

[10] T.L. Gibson, "Wholeness and transcendence in the practice of pastoral psychotherapy from a Judaeo Christian perspective" in P. Young-Eisendrath and M.E. Miller (eds.), *The Psychology of Mature Spirituality* (Philadelphia: Routledge, 2000), 175–86.

[11] W. Popkes, "New Testament principles of wholeness: (and spiritual growth)," *Evangelical Quarterly* 64 (1992), 319–32.

[12] R. Beuchner, "Journey toward Wholeness," *Theology Today* 49 (1993), 4: 454–64.

[13] Goldbrunner, *Holiness.*

[14] G.W. Moon, "A personal journey to spiritually sensitive psychotherapy: An interview with David G. Benner," *Journal of Psychology and Christianity* 21 (2002), 1:64–71, 68.

[15] R. Hurding, *Pathways to Wholeness: Pastoral care in a postmodern age* (London: Hodder & Stoughton, 1998).

[16] J.J. Chriss (ed.), *Counseling and the Therapeutic State* (New York: Aldine de Gruyter, 1999); F. Furedi, "The silent ascendancy of therapeutic culture in Britain," *Society* 39 (2002), 3:16–24.

[17] D.M. Henderson, *John Wesley's Class Meeting: A model for making disciples* (Nappanee, Ind.: Evangel Publishing House, 1997), 102.

[18] Henderson, *Class Meeting,* 119.

[19] R. Davis and G. Rupp (eds.), *A History of the Methodist Church in Great Britain* (London: Epworth Press, 1965).

[20] Henderson, *Class Meeting,* 103ff.

[21] D. Drakeford, *Integrity Therapy* (Waco, Tex.: Broadman Press, 1967).

[22] Henderson, *Class Meeting,* 119.

[23] Holmes and Williams, *Changed Lives,* and Holmes, *Trinity.*

[24] Holmes and Williams, *Changed Lives.*

[25] E.H. Peterson, *The Message: The Bible in contemporary language* (Colorado Springs: Navpress, 2002), 1,920.

[26] Middlemiss, *Experience,* 245.

[27] J.H. Boyd, *Reclaiming the Soul: The search for meaning in a self-centered culture* (Cleveland, Ohio: The Pilgrim Press, 1996), 50.

[28] Furedi, "Therapeutic culture."

[29] R. May, "The problem of will, decision and responsibility in psychological health," *The Christian Scholar* 66 (1963), 3:235–44.

[30] Chriss (ed.), *Counseling,* 3ff.

[31] Chriss (ed.), *Counseling,* iix.

Qualities of Christ-Likeness:
Your Relationships with Others

Love is at the heart of the gospel. How we treat others must therefore be firmly at the heart of our Christ-likeness journey. Later we will look specifically at family relationships, but in this group of qualities we explore what changes Christ-likeness will bring in our capacity to love others. The pattern of friendships and capacity for relationships is another area where male and female are frequently quite different. Men often have fewer friendships, but those they have are likely to carry a deep loyalty. Women often have a wider circle of friends and place more importance on spending time with others. In a Christ-like journey we will learn from each other about how to grow a variety of friendships.

A love for people and a passion to give life

You have become a lover of people. You no longer blame others, find fault with them or carry anger against them. People are no longer an intrusion in your life. You have the capacity to enjoy the company of anyone you spend time with, and to give them life. At the end of a conversation you know you have given something of yourself and something of the Lord. You are aware that the person or people you were with have drunk at your well. You feel drained, but lifted, aware that it was the grace of Christ that gave you that moment. This is Christ-likeness.

Able to put others first

You have allowed Christ and others to meet your needs, so are able to live putting Christ and others first. You value the range of perspectives others bring, especially when different from yours. You are able to listen to others and see things from their point of view, with empathy and support. You give yourself 1,000 per cent in all relationships, and hear from the Lord as to how He would want to affirm the person. You show in your life a capacity to love others, even the unlovely aspects of their lives, while not condoning sin. You do not fear others becoming greater than you, as that promotes the Kingdom of God. This is Christ-likeness.

Honor and faithfulness in all relationships

You value long and deep relationships. Friendships of a lifetime you value especially highly. You have a deep sense of the worth of writing history together with others. You are able to think long term in any situation. No encounter is a once off, a single moment, but is part of a long life together. Such friendships you seek to protect, and they are not ever lost because of lack of commitment on your part. Only time and distance constrain such ongoing friendships. It does not matter whether your friend is a man or a woman, you communicate that they are important to you, and that you wish honor and faithfulness to be at the heart of all your relationships. This is Christ-likeness.

An ability to communicate

Christ had all the spiritual gifts He needed. These included the ability to teach, to express Himself, even emotionally, and the capacity to meet anyone where they were. Each person who came would have been instantly aware that He was looking at them. He was meeting them. He was connecting with them. But it never stopped there. He was able to read their spirit and their body language. He could clearly identify what was true and what was untrue in what they said to Him. He delighted in people and in communication with them at every level. His whole nature reached out to them, engaged with them and enjoyed their company. Whoever he was talking to was at that moment the most important person in His life, and they both knew it. He had developed the ability to chat to anyone about almost anything. He knew the key question to ask, while being aware of what people were feeling when they began to tell Him about themselves. Likewise, you have begun to experience these capacities and yearn for them to increase. This is Christ-likeness.

A capacity to read and listen to other people

As a student of human nature, you have reached a place where you are beginning to understand the 70 per cent of any conversation that is not spoken. You sense what people are thinking and feeling, as well as saying. Much of the time you are aware of two conversations taking place, one with words and another from the spirit, and you are able to place equal emphasis on both. So you gain a deep understanding of who people really are and what they really feel, as well as think. You have become aware of the contradictions between their head and their heart. You know what people need to do to own the hidden side of themselves. You become a mirror for them of how the Lord is really closer than a brother to all they are. This is Christ-likeness.

You love others as they are, but require change

> There is no compromise. There is no alternative. You just have to say what you hear the Lord saying. But as you say it, it is seasoned and mellowed by the sweetness of His Spirit and yours. So as it is said it has the power to go very deep, finding the richest soil in the other person, telling them clearly that this is very important. As you met them you loved them, so they knew they were accepted before you spoke. Though you always wait for confirmation of their permission and God's, before speaking, you are able to lead them into a journey of change, as God and others have led you. This is Christ-likeness.

Being righteously offensive

> Christ had a difficult side to His nature, a side that was salty, just as He taught we all should have. You have experienced this in your own relationships and have learnt through practice to be offensive in a righteous way. You have let God offend you, pointing out your faults, and have valued the clarity that such offence brings. Where invited, you take time to help others see not only what is wrong but also how to put it right. You ensure that support is on hand and that discipline is always accompanied by affirmation. This is Christ-likeness.

You have enemies

> You are not afraid of having enemies. You know the Master has told us, "If they persecuted me, they will persecute you also" (Jn. 15:20). Having such enemies is a compliment to you from the Enemy. So while seeking to live at peace with all, you have accepted that some will choose to remain enemies. You have learnt to manage the

resulting confrontation with a combination of humility and authority. It is all part of the spiritual landscape, part of your daily life. Christ had enemies, but unlike us, none were of His own making. Just being the Son of God was enough. The lines were drawn, the battle was engaged, and although He never lost a round, not even in the grave, He did have a lifelong battle on His hands. He fought both the Enemy, and the Enemy's friends. This is Christ-likeness.

Your company is enjoyed and valued

You are able to enjoy your own company in a way that you never have done before. But in another sense, you never seem to have a moment free because your company is enjoyed by others. You can do both, aloneness and togetherness. You know your popularity is about Jesus in you, about bringing others to feast at His table. This is Christ-likeness.

You are honored by both sexes

You are not just a man's man, or not just one of the girls. People of both genders value your company and know they can trust you. As a man, men and women honor you. As a woman, men and women honor you. They have seen and benefited from the life you have given them, for you give them Christ. This is Christ-likeness.

Our Human Search
for Authentic Spirituality

At the core of our living in wholeness in Christ is our spiritual nature and spiritual reality. Christ-likeness is formed in us not by what we do, but by who we are and who we are becoming. This ever-changing lifelong journey engages the whole of our human make-up, our body–spirit unity. But it also introduces us to the spiritual world.

Maybe because of psychology's denial of our spiritual nature, or our fear of the devil and the spiritual world, we have as Christians been guilty of shying away from these areas. They have been relegated by many to another time and another reality. They are not thought to be relevant to us now. We have lost touch both with the immediacy of human spirit as part of our nature now, and also with spiritual reality as the dwelling place of God. Yet if we are to do a Christ-like journey, we need to be introduced to both by the Lord, because wholeness requires that we be at ease with both the spiritual world, and our own remarkable spiritual nature. A consciousness of Christ-in-us-in-spiritual-reality needs to fill the whole of our life and our nature. So what is spirituality? How should we understand the spiritual world?

Introducing Spiritual Reality

Within the Church very little has been written about human spirit, even though there are many references to it in Scripture.[1] In some Church circles even to talk about human spirit would invoke the charge of being New Age! Such a reaction shows the level of ignorance that there still is in the Church about this subject, and the lack of helpful teaching.[2] This failing inhibits our understanding of a practical personal spirituality as a valid relational aspect of our Christ-like journey. For instance, when thinking of our own human nature, how many of us are aware that the Hebrew concept of body–spirit unity (Gen. 2:7) gives a holistic view of human make-up and suggests that all parts of our nature are damaged by sin, and fragmented by its baggage?

The Biblical concept of body–spirit unity also suggests a spiritual side to our personal human nature *now*. It is important to argue for the centrality of our spiritual nature, as modern psychology has traditionally not recognized this, preferring instead a mind–body dualism. Hebrew body–spirit unity suggests an equality, a co-mingling within ourselves of both spirit and body, rather than a spiritually good "core" to our bad physical nature, as the Greeks saw it. When we see our spiritual nature as part of our whole being, we can also see in our spiritual nature some of the more subliminal explanations of the damage in our lives.

The concept of human spirit as the image-of-God-in-us sets humanity apart from other species and all material reality. Implicit in the suggestion that we are in God's image, having spirit-body uniqueness, is the deep value of each human being. This also suggests the possibility that we can all be greater than who we now are, which in turn helps to release us from the constraints of our human circumstances. We should be encouraged by this to seek out the blockages, and bring to God the tarnished image, with all its redeemable potential in relationships with ourselves, others and God.

But human spirit also reaches beyond us, suggesting not only the possibility of a supernatural life for every person, but also of our being able to connect with others at more subliminal levels than mere words and body language. It suggests that as we relate to others, at least two stories exist between us: not merely our relationality at a verbal and physical level, but also at a spiritual level, and, for Christians, at the level of our spiritual nature in Christ. This idea is particularly helpful when considering relationships between men and women. It often explains sources of emotional and spiritual conflict that are not normally seen or heard.

Finally, with the help of the idea of a social Trinity, and through our human spirit, we can more easily believe that we are able to hear and know God, who is a spiritual being. This helps us envisage the "platform" of our human spiritual nature being a "contact point" with the Trinity community. For many of us, human spirit "after the image of God" suggests a prehistory where He has a part in giving us this image, willing us to be created and born. This in turn suggests the potential of a forthcoming eternity in which we engage this God whose image we mirror. So what is this spirituality?

Defining Spirituality

The need for a definition of contemporary spirituality first became obvious to me (Peter) some years ago when trying to define what it meant to be human and spiritual in the modern world. Although definitions of spirituality do exist in the Church,[3] after much research I decided to adopt one from outside the Church, a definition with a more clinical and therapeutic aspect to it. One that came closest to what I was looking for was Martsolf and Mickley's, which noted five central *features* of spirituality.[4] The authors have combined the ideas of several modern theorists, none of them specifically Christian. The five features are:

1. *Meaning*: the ontological (essence of our being) and significance of life; making sense of life situations; deriving purpose in existence.
2. *Value*: beliefs and standards that are cherished; having to do with truth, beauty, worth of a thought, object or behavior; often discussed as "ultimate values."
3. *Transcendence*: experience and appreciation of a dimension beyond the self; expanding self-boundaries.
4. *Connecting*: relationships with self, others, God/higher power, and the environment.
5. *Becoming*: an unfolding of life that demands reflection and experience; includes, among other things, a sense of who one is and how one knows.

What is immediately obvious in this explanation of spirituality is that all the features are practical and useful. They have a hands-on pragmatism that is sometimes lacking within the Church. For instance, few Christian definitions of spirituality even mention personal change. Nonetheless, these ideas are entirely compatible with the understanding of Christ-likeness as a journey, and our becoming more human as Christ is formed in us. Each of these five features, or characteristics of spirituality describes a movement toward something more meaningful, something that can be identified, possessed and developed by the individual. Each area is also accommodating of the person, seeking to connect with the individual regardless of creed, doctrine or personal perspective. Together they form a landscape of key attributes of spirituality.

Perhaps because they were drawn from research in nursing, the features are also specific, and are written in straightforward language that can be easily understood and appropriated. They encourage us to think through our ultimate values, and thereby grow in our own spirituality, and to identify aspects of our lives that lack meaning, or where we may have "lost" our spirituality.

This definition is a broad "working" model, not confined to personal private ideas of spiritual reality. It recognizes communal connectedness and a sense of that which is beyond self, thereby creating opportunities for new learning and change. It notes a sense of becoming who one really is, and could be, in a relational setting. This descriptive landscape implies there is an intrinsic, authentic and transforming spirituality at the core of human personhood.

We must remember that these five features of spirituality are written from outside the Church. They are entirely coherent with a Biblical idea of human spirit and spiritual reality, but they are not ideal and more work is needed to find contemporary Biblical equivalents. What is evident is that spiritual reality, the way these two researchers see it, is not the home of the demonic or of witchcraft. Likewise, spiritual reality should not be condemned or feared by the Church. After all, it is where God dwells. On many occasions, those who started their spiritual journey from these non-Christian perspectives have discovered Christ on their journey.

Introducing Contemporary Spirituality

Christian spirituality is Christ-centered and is fundamental to our journey into Christ-likeness. But outside the Church there is an increasing interest in human spirituality. Belief in an authentic, tangible, spiritual reality is becoming more widespread. Though as followers of Christ our spirituality is unapologetically distinct. If we are to grow in our capacity to discern good and evil in spiritual and material reality, it is helpful for us to be familiar with spiritualities that lie outside the Church.

Hay and Hunt, researching spirituality among the UK unchurched, notes a significant numerical growth – from 29 per cent in 1987, to 55 per cent in 2000 – in those who believe that spirituality is grounded in their personal experience, while those admitting an awareness of evil rose from 12 per cent to 25 per cent.[5] In our lifetime we have moved from a place where it was unfashionable to talk about spiritual reality ("what ain't seen ain't real"), to a culture in the early twenty-first century in which, at least in non-Christian society, it is increasingly acceptable to speak of one's spirituality, personal journey and experiences.[6] We would refer you to other authors and my (Peter's) own writings to get a more thorough background to the question of where such interest does and does not lie.[7]

In some fields of psychology spirituality is now a significant area of research.[8] A spiritless twentieth-century psychology is now awakening to the fact that we are more than our biology, having a capacity, experience and hunger for supra-sensible reality.[9] Also in psychology, the measure of intelligence quotient (IQ), gave rise to EQ (emotional intelligence), which has now led into SQ (spiritual intelligence).[10] In this book we are suggesting that all three are essential on the journey to become more Christ-like by becoming more fully human.

Nursing is leading the way in promoting the rise of spirituality in health care, where there is a call for an awakening of spirit in clinical practice,[11] and recognition of spiritual distress and how to work with it.[12] There is also a growing body of evidence that spirituality is a key health contributor,[13] in some circles becoming known as "spiritual health."[14] Psychological therapies are one example of an area where spirituality has become a key element.[15]

Such spiritualities are seen as having a transformative character, being personally experienced and relationally celebrated. Very little of this new thinking is being driven by the Church, although the pastoral emphasis on wholeness does lay a useful foundation for incorporating spirituality into health.

The modern failure of materialism and the rise of secularism have also played their part in the renewed search for spirituality. For instance, one of the biggest factors may be the breakdown of community.[16] Society has been fragmenting socially and relationally for several hundred years or more. Many believe that spirituality has a key part to play in the recovery process as people find each other in common interests and purpose. Jesus taught the need for such belonging two thousand years ago, so it is particularly tragic that in the twenty-first century these new expressions of spirituality are emphasizing these values while the Church largely is not.

In educational discourse the idea of spirituality has re-emerged in the UK as an important element in schooling. National Curriculum documentation describes pupil attainment as consisting of learning, achievement *and* personal development (which incorporates spiritual, moral, social and cultural development). Such statutory assessments of spiritual development are fuelling the debate about spirituality, calling for a new language, new methodology and a means of supporting personal and communal spirituality. Fullan, for instance, used the language of spirituality interchangeably with the language of "moral purpose."[17]

Likewise, in the field of business we now "talk spiritual." Referring to the American corporate scene, Mitroff and Dentron note that most people have strong spiritual beliefs, regardless of religion.[18] They also argue that where company and spiritual values coalesce, company performance is higher. Roof also comments that spirituality is firmly entrenched in the marketplace.[19] Here in the UK, articles on spirituality in business are common, as is the emphasis on ethical leadership.[20] Coupled with this are the advertising media, where "spirit" and "spirituality" are often mentioned.

Many other disciplines, such as gender studies, theoretical physics, feng shui[21] and even gardening design (e.g. the Chelsea Flower Show) are all "talking spiritual." Motor mechanics and fishing can now be spiritual acts, as can studying the biodiversity of the natural world. The construction of Ground Zero is also being conceived as the building of a spiritual place.[22] Overall, several features of this spirituality emerge, in particular its unevenness and non-religious pretensions. Yet amidst this enthusiasm we still have no unified understanding of what spirituality is.[23]

Where Is this Transforming Spirituality in the Church?

Change characterizes contemporary Western culture, and what we are noting is that part of this change has been a unique search for human spirituality in a relational and often in a professional context. Spirituality in past centuries has been the domain of religion, but not any longer. Outside of established religion we are seeing a significant rise in interest in spirituality, though not led by the New Age fringe, but within mainstream academic and professional life. If it is to respond to this international movement, the Church needs a greater understanding both of itself and of contemporary trends in spirituality.

We are not denying that mature types of spirituality do exist in the Church – Ignatian, Quaker and Celtic spiritualities, for example. Francis Schaeffer was one of the first Christian thinkers to put the subject of contemporary spirituality on the modern map within the Church.[24] For me (Peter), however, it was the Old Testament scholar Harry Ellison who, in 1969, first introduced me to the Hebrew idea of body–spirit unity. At the heart of this contemporary interest in spirituality is the idea of personal journeying and positive change, both of which the Church has largely lost from its own practices. So people who desire to explore themselves, relationships and the world they live in are left to make the journey without Christ.

What we have been noting is that there are few constructs for a clinical transformational spirituality within the modern Western Church. This contrasts with Martsolf and Mickley's tangible spirituality that is assumed to be part of both human make-up and its therapeutic change process. Within a nursing context, growing in spirituality is part of personal healing, with change assumed to be at its core. People are committed to both learning and positive change.

It sometimes feels as though, just as psychology and its therapies have hijacked from the Church much of the worth and identity of the human search for wholeness and healing, so this contemporary outside-of-religion spirituality is likewise showing the Church what people today want on their spiritual journey. The Church is in danger of being left with a static and intangible spirituality that contemporary people find neither attractive nor transforming. As Christians, we are presenting to the unchurched majority a spirituality that is mostly historic in nature, taught academically and not seen in a positive way. This is in marked contrast to the type of spirituality we are describing in this book. The spirituality we are talking about requires a Christ-likeness that must overflow into every area of our lives, unapologetically yielding personal and relational wholeness. At its heart it is transformative.

Of course, the Church has not got it all wrong. In writings on the spiritual disciplines, for example, it has emphasized a spirituality that can deeply enrich a person's relationship with Christ. As an example, we would like to end the chapter with a review of just one area of Christian spirituality that has all the transformative power anyone can handle – spiritual gifting as we find it in Scripture. Any cluster of such gifts will give both innovative and transforming spirituality. The giving and exercising of such a range of gifts is unique to Christianity.

Spiritual Gifts from God

The ultimate gift for all of us from the Father is the Son Jesus Christ. He in turn gave us the Holy Spirit. But Christ also gave us spiritual gifts through the Holy Spirit, helping open communication between the two worlds, the material and spiritual. The suggestion from Scripture is that all of us have spiritual gifting, and that we should become more proficient in these spiritual gifts as we mature.

This gifting is fundamentally relational, being given "for the common good." Rather than experiencing just a bit of success on the odd occasion, we should all expect to live with such anointing and its spiritual gifting. As we mature in Christ-likeness, we will be able to take personal responsibility for growing in these expressions of our spirituality. Let us close the chapter with a list of some of these gifts. Which ones would you like from the Lord?

Administration/management	1 Cor. 12:28
Anointing/baptism in the Holy Spirit	1 Cor. 12:12–13
Apostleship	Eph. 4:11; 1 Cor. 12:28
Celibacy	1 Cor. 7:7–8
Comforting/consoling	Ps. 94:19; 2 Cor. 1:4–5
Creating wealth/almsgiving	Rom. 12:8
Discerning spirits	1 Cor. 12:10
Encouragement/exhortation	Rom. 12:8
Evangelism	Eph. 4:11
Faith	1 Cor. 12:8–10
Fathering	1 Cor 4:14ff.; Phlm. 10; 1 Tim. 1:2,18, etc.
Healing	1 Cor. 12:9,28,30
Helps	1 Cor. 12:28
Hospitality	1 Pet. 4:9–10
Interpretation of dreams	Acts 2:17
Knowledge (intellectual/ spiritual)	1 Cor. 12:8
Leadership	Rom. 12:8
Martyrdom	1 Cor. 13:3
Mercy	Rom. 12:8
Missionary/church planting	Eph. 3:6–8
Music, song-writing, poetry	Eph. 5:19; Psalms/Psalter
Power, signs, miracles	Rom. 15:19; 1 Cor. 12:10,28
Prayer/intercession	1 Cor. 14:14; Eph. 6:18
Preaching	Acts 16:6
Prophecy	Rom. 12:6; 1 Cor. 12:10; Eph. 4:11
Seer/visionary/dreamer	Gen. 37:19; Dan. 7:1; Mt. 1:20
Service/serving/servant-hood	Rom. 12:7
Shepherding/pastor	Eph. 4:11
Teaching	Rom. 12:7; 1 Cor. 12:28; Eph. 4:11
Tongues/interpretation	1 Cor. 12:10; 14:27–28
Voluntary poverty	1 Cor. 13:3
Wisdom	1 Cor. 12:8
Worship/Song of the Lord	Jn. 4:24; Rom. 12:1; Phil. 3:3

Notes

[1] In the NIV concordance there are over 120 clear references to human spirit, alongside Holy Spirit and other spirits.

[2] That being said, there are some good books, though mostly out of print, that do introduce the subject. See, for instance, A.B. Come, *Human Spirit and Holy Spirit* (Philadelphia: The Westminster Press, 1959); C.A. van Peursen, *Body, Soul, Spirit: A survey of the body–mind problem* (London: Oxford University Press, 1966); J.H. Robb, *Man as Infinite Spirit* (Milwaukee: Marquette University Publications, 1974); Boyd, *Soul*; K. Nicholson, *Body and Soul: The transcendence of materialism* (Boulder, Colo.: Westview Press, 1997); W.S. Brown (ed.), *Whatever Happened to the Soul? Scientific and theological portraits of human nature* (Minneapolis: Augsburg Fortress, 1998); E.L. Johnson, "Whatever Happened to the Human Soul? A brief Christian genealogy of a psychological term," *Journal of Psychology and Theology, Special Issue: Perspectives on the Self/Soul* 26 (1998), 1:16–28, etc. Come is still my favourite.

[3] S. Armirtham and R.J. Pryor, *The Invitation to the Feast of Life: Resources for spiritual formation in theological education* (Geneva: World Council of Churches, Programme on Theological Education, 1991).

[4] D.S. Martsolf and J.R. Mickley, "The concept of spirituality in nursing theories: differing world-views and extent of focus," *Journal of Advanced Nursing* 27 (1998), 294–303.

[5] D. Hay and K. Hunt, *Understanding the Spirituality of People who don't go to Church* (Nottingham: Nottingham University Press, 2000).

[6] J. Drane, *Rebuilding the Household of Faith: Being spiritual, human and Christian in today's world* (2002, online). Available from <www.ctbi.org.uk/assembly/Drane.doc> (accessed 29 February 2004).

[7] S. Savage, S. Collins-Mayo, B. Mayo and G. Cray, *Making Sense of Generation Y: The world view of 15- to 25-year-olds* (London: Church House Publishing, 2006); P.R. Holmes, "Spirituality: some disciplinary perspectives" in K. Flanagan and P.C. Jupp (eds.), *The Sociology of Spirituality* (Ashgate, 2007).

[8] Young-Eisendrath and Miller (eds.), *Psychology*.

[9] A.C. Purton, "Unconditional positive regard and its spiritual implications" in B. Thorne and E. Lambers (eds.), *Person Centred Therapy: A European perspective* (London: Sage, 1998), 23–37.

[10] D. Zohar and I. Marshall, *SQ: Spiritual intelligence: the ultimate intelligence* (London: Bloomsbury Publishing, 2000)

[11] M.A. Burkhardt and M.G. Nagai-Jacobson, "Reawakening spirit in clinical practice," *Journal of Holistic Nursing* 12 (1994), 1:9–21.

[12] P. Burnard, "Spiritual distress and the nursing response," *Journal of Advanced Nursing* 12 (1987), 377–82.

[13] H.G. Koenig, "Religion, spirituality and medicine: a rebuttal to skeptics," *International Journal of Psychiatry in Religion* 29 (1999), 2:123–31.

[14] T.J. O'Connor, "Review of quantity and types of spirituality research in three health care databases (1962–1999): implications for the health care ministry," *Journal of Pastoral Care and Counseling* 56 (2002), 3:227–32.

[15] T.E. Clark and M. Thompson, "Psychology and spirituality: meeting at the boundaries," *The Way Supplement* 69 (1990), 29–42; R.E. Fouch, *What is the experience of spirituality within psychotherapy? A heuristic study of seven psychotherapists' experience of spirituality within psychotherapy*, Dissertation (The Union Institution, USA, 1997); D.A. Steere, *Spiritual Presence in Psychotherapy: A guide for care-givers* (New York: Brunner-Mazelle, 1997); R.C. Schwartz, "Releasing the soul: psychotherapy as a spiritual practice" in F. Walsh (ed.), *Spiritual Resources in Family Therapy* (New York: Guilford Publications, 1999); S. Izzard, "Holding contradictions together: an object relational view of healthy spirituality," *Contact* 140 (2003), 1:2–8.

[16] A. Etzioni, *The Spirit of Community: Rights, responsibilities and the communitarian agenda* (London: Fontana Press, 1995).

[17] M. Fullan, *Change Forces: The sequel* (Philadelphia: Routledge Falmer, 1999).

[18] I.I. Mitroff and E.A. Dentron, *A Spiritual Audit of Corporate America: A hard look at spirituality, religion and values in the workplace* (San Francisco: Jossey-Bass, 1999).

[19] W.C. Roof, *Spiritual Marketplace: Baby-boomers and the remaking of American religion* (Princeton, N.J.: Princeton University Press, 1999).

[20] S.R. Covey, "Principles hold key to leadership success," *Professional Manager* 41 (September 2001), 29–30; Goleman, *Leaders*,

[21] G. Gunn, *Office Feng Shui* (Abingdon: Hodder & Stoughton, 1999).

[22] T. Conran, "Solemn Witness: A pilgrimage to Ground Zero at the World Trade Center," *Journal of Systemic Therapies* 21 (2002), 3:39–47.

[23] Some have begun this work. See, for instance, V.L. Schermer, *Spirit and Psyche: a new paradigm for psychology, psychoanalysis and psychotherapy* (London: Jessica Kingsley, 2003).

[24] F.A. Schaeffer, *True Spirituality* (London: Hodder & Stoughton, 1972).

Qualities of Christ-Likeness:
Our Spirituality

For all of us, our spirituality is an area of major change during our journey into Christ-likeness. Some, most often women, will have been quite sensitive spiritually before becoming Christians and might embrace this truth more easily. Others of us have been quite closed to the reality of the spiritual world. Once living as Christians, we often try to manage our faith cognitively and intellectually, remaining quite separated from God's view of spirituality. Yet Christ-likeness demands that all of us actively explore this area of our lives.

Conscious of your own spiritual nature

You have developed an awareness that you are much more than your biology. You are body and spirit, and know that both are essential God-given parts of you and your view of the world. You know your spirit, and this has deepened your knowing of Holy Spirit and spiritual reality. You appreciate this part of who you are and have integrated it within every area of your life and relationships. This is Christ-likeness.

Aware of spiritual reality

You are aware of human spirit and Holy Spirit. Spiritual reality is rather like a parallel world that you are now actively part of. You are also aware of spirit in others, and spiritual reality in and around you and them. Like you, others communicate from their intellect and their body and spirit. This further complicates the avalanche of information that you are getting, but you are able to distinguish and discern what is being received, spirit to spirit, just as Christ did. You know what talks to you from your mind, and what talks to you from your spirit. But while you are aware of these distinctives, you have also moved on to no longer distinguishing them. It is a natural flow. This is Christ-likeness.

At ease in both worlds

You are at ease in both worlds and live in both all the time. But when you move in and out of spiritual reality it is God's grace. For you know that you cannot fully do so yet. He constrains our exposure and knowledge to this aspect of His reality. He will always let us learn enough, but we will never know more than we need. You know that you are being trusted with more because you are becoming increasingly trustworthy. This is Christ-likeness.

You are also aware that the Enemy does not dominate the spiritual world. Instead, spiritual reality is where God dwells. He is the creator of all of this, as well as creator of material reality. Dying in Christ is now merely graduating, moving on into God. It is not another fearful battle, a dark unknown. You know you will give up the one in order to more fully embrace the other. This is Christ-likeness.

Naturally exercising a range of spiritual gifting

Moving in and out of spiritual gifting is no longer a novelty. You view it as a necessity, as a way of life. You do not need to identify each gift individually, or notice specifically when you are exercising the gifts. They have become part of your daily life. You breathe in life and you breathe out Christ. He is the true gift for everyone. This is Christ-likeness.

Able to live in openness of spirit

You know how to live in openness to the Lord and to others from your spirit. You now do this consistently. Others feel this welcome; they feel accepted. Not only are you open, discernment has also given you the practiced capacity to trawl the landscape, picking up all kinds of things. But you are also past this novel stage, to a place where you are sifting out most of what you find, ignoring it, closing it down, to focus on what you need to know. Christ is your source, by His Spirit. This is Christ-likeness.

Able to close your spirit

You know the times when, like David, you need to close your spirit to others and the Enemy. You know how and when to wear your armor and keep your shield up. You can do this intuitively. You can close your spirit to the damage, letting it bounce off you, without necessarily rejecting the person. You can give the person the opportunity to engage in relationship righteously, to separate themselves from the damage, as you have. This is Christ-likeness.

An unconquerable spirit

You have a supernatural tenacity, a spiritual resolve, which allows you to rise above what is intended to swamp and overpower you. You also allow the Lord to restore your spirit, even in the battle while you are being assaulted. You cannot stop the Enemy attacking, but you can stop the damage. This happens intuitively, subliminally, without your ever needing to think about it. This is Christ-likeness.

Not living in fear of the Enemy

You do not fear the Enemy, but are aware of how he is able to manipulate fallen, damaged human nature, how he can perpetrate evil and harm through others and by others. You do not believe the lie that what he does is more powerful than anything God can do. You know Christ as Redeemer and frequently experience His supernatural redemption in your life, and the lives of others. This is Christ-likeness.

8

Obstacles to Becoming Christ-Like

In the previous chapter we defined Christ-likeness as a journey whereby Christ is more fully formed in us, but also as a journey in which we must all actively participate. It would be nice to think it was a gentle, gradual and inevitable part of our growing experience of being a Christian. But the truth, in some ways, is the opposite. Christ-likeness is a rare commodity in most churches and many of us struggle deeply because of its lack. So to ensure that we are properly equipped for this journey we must look at some of the obstacles that stand in our path – first, in this chapter, in a general sense, then, in the following chapter, at a more personal level.

A Hebrew View of Sin and Repentance

Yahweh places importance on wholeness change (e.g. Ex. 33:5; Ps. 32:8–9; 55:19; Acts 11:5ff.), as does contemporary spirituality, as we have seen. When Christians refuse to change in response to God's voice and wish, they are therefore refusing to harmonize their lives with Christ, with *imago Dei* wholeness. Keifer suggested that there was probably only one element of Jewish religion that was unique: the idea of sin.[1] This Hebrew idea has in turn given Christianity this unique feature.

All of us are beset by sin. It is inevitable, because we are living in a fallen damaged world. You may be one of those remarkable people who successfully resist temptation and live godly lives. Well done! But Scripture is clear. According to Biblical teaching, none of us is without sin in this life. That means that an ongoing experience of repentance should be part of our daily experience.

Repentance is our willingness to "turn around," change and do things differently. But in the Old Testament there is a consistent sense that sin is a refusal to change in a positive Christ-like way. It took me several years to realize this from Scripture, although it now seems so obvious. Relationship with Christ, and becoming more like Him, mean we are all called to personal change. But something in all of us refuses to change. It is our sin. It is the obstacle we all face in our journey toward Christ-likeness. Sin dries out the dough so it cannot be kneaded.

Two Hebrew words describe the repentance to which we are all called: *nacham*, to lament, grieve, be sorry, change one's mind; and *shub*, to turn back, to return.[2] Christ took up this key theme at the beginning of His ministry (Mt. 4:17), and was still emphasizing it toward the end of His life (Lk. 24:46–47). On most pages of Hebrew Scripture we see a record of Yahweh requiring change or repentance from Israel. His self-disclosure as the living God meant that His people had to choose either to follow His ways, or suffer the consequences of the sin of not changing. See, for instance, Leviticus 26:1–13 and 14–39, where the author outlines the reward for obedience followed by the punishment for disobedience. These choices are clearly seen from the beginning of Jewish history (Gen. 17:9ff.; 22:15–18, etc.). The reason is that damaged, fallen people all need to learn positively both a change of mind and a change of lifestyle. If they do not change, they are in a place of sin against the wishes of Yahweh.

In suggesting the concept of sin as an integral part of the Christ-likeness journey, we are drawing on a long tradition in both the Church[3] and Scripture (e.g. Prov. 5:22; Mt. 12:31; Rom. 6:23, etc.). When we suggest that sin can be seen as a refusal to repent or change, we are borrowing from Boman's Hebrew perspective that sin against God and ourselves is in essence our unwillingness to change.[4] As McFadyen says: "Sin is the resistance or opposition to the energies of God's dynamic order, the disorientation of personal energies in an alternative dynamic, a distortion of the conditions of genuine joy."[5]

Today in the Church the traditional view of sin (Gk. *hamartia*, "missing the mark") is that it is "the lack of conformity to the moral law of God, either in act, disposition, or state."[6] This definition suggests that all actions may be seen as either sinful or righteous. But we may deduce from Hebrew thought that sin is our personal, stubborn, unwillingness to change (Ps. 55:19b), our refusal to seek authentically to mirror Him in the desire to conform more closely to His moral character.

We should note at this point, of course, that most of us are quite unaware of our refusal to change. In fact, many of us have sought change for years. We haven't ever deliberately chosen to refuse to repent. If someone had shown us what to do, we would have done it many years ago. God understands the weaknesses we have been struggling against and doesn't judge us for what we did not know. But He wants to equip all of us to move on in our Christ-likeness, to grow in our capacity to change, to become more of who He created us to be. If we are now willing to start welcoming the kneading, then those invisible obstacles need be obstacles no longer.

Sin is humanity's desire to *be*, rather than to *become*.[7] Human nature continues to be, to refuse to change, rather than to become, for example, to become like Christ, whereas Christ requires everyone to change to be like Him. What is clear both from Scripture, and to students of human nature, is that people do not like some types of change, especially the kind that requires painful positive behavior and adjustment. This is true in even simple things such as exercising, eating more healthily, no longer succumbing to addictions, etc.

The basis of the Christian view of sin is our need to repent of it, to "turn around," to go in the opposite direction. Our refusal to do this when the Holy Spirit points to areas of sin in our lives blocks our path to becoming both mature and more like Christ. To be more authentically human, to be more like Christ, mirroring the vibrant harmonic *perichoresis* of Trinity, is to be in a permanent state of becoming. We no longer need to remain in a stubborn, unchanging place of being. To mature in Christ we need to experience ongoing continual positive change within a learning relationship that includes social Trinity, ourselves and others. Our base human nature, wishing for a quiet life, is permanently in a default position, expressing (perhaps unknowingly) a stubborn unwillingness to change. In contrast, a Holy Spirit "quickened" human nature, either driven by human need (e.g. awareness of compulsions or sin), or desiring to go deeper in allegiance to Christ, will increasingly mirror God.

The Church's idea of "original sin" could similarly be seen not only as damage to every part of our nature, but simply as our disinclination to change, our refusal to align ourselves with a Christ-centered sanctifying process of positive change. Sadly, the inclination to oppose any process of change is embedded in all of us. By an exercise of will, however, we can take responsibility for ourselves, and can make the choice to harmonize self with Christ and others in this journey process of change. A contemporary view of human nature sees it less as sinful and more as flawed. This still fits, as none of us, either inside or outside the Church, are who we could or should be.[8] Wholeness means completing what is lacking, being willing to change.

Sin and Wholeness

The Old Testament is full of examples of the stubborn refusal to change. Most of the founders and leaders of Israel showed this kind of sin, either resisting God's will or not obeying Him in the way He required. Solomon, for instance, by not separating himself from the kingdoms and pagan gods around him, refused to conform to Yahweh's wishes. Uxoriousness, as it is called, was the pattern of Solomon's life. He conformed to the kingdoms around him by taking foreign wives and adopting their gods into a pantheon of gods in Jerusalem. This refusal to align himself to Yahweh's wish that the nation should be distinguished by the worship of one God ultimately caused the downfall of Solomon's kingdom (1 Kgs. 11:1ff.).

For Paul, faith in Christ releases the potential we all have for a new self-understanding in this present life (Rom. 10:5–21; Gal. 2:20; Phil. 3:7–11, etc.). This is the beginning of finding Christ, finding greater wholeness and personhood. Paul sees salvation *beginning* in this life. As David Ford suggests, salvation can be health for all of us now.[9]

We need to develop a new understanding of ourselves based on God's perspective, a "single-mindedness" that helps us focus on what obstructs the formation of Christ in us. Our self-deceit and its sin needs to be exposed. Our stubborn dis-informed view of ourselves that blocks our path to wholeness has to be challenged by God, not just by a therapist or pastor. Without such understanding from God, a Christian has very little reason to change. If our Christian life is limited to learning about God, then apart from attending church more often and adopting godly pursuits, there is little we can do. But God is offering to be our diagnostician, to talk to us about us. "The gospel is the gospel or good news of the Kingdom, of the reign of God breaking into, transforming and renewing this world-order of sin, decay and death."[10]

In letting go of our pasts and their darkness, we become capable of moving into permanent positive deep change (Ps. 85:8–9). As Lambourne suggests, wholeness can only occur in relationships that include God, our own personal and spiritual natures, and the support of others.[11]

What we are talking about here is a theology of positive Christ-like change. Such a theology of positive change, as Lee observes, is something the Church has not yet written. Emanating from such a theology, salvation becomes a process of God's continual redeeming creativity within vibrant, Christ-centered community relationships.[12] We become more authentically human by learning a perpetual journey of becoming who we were created to be in Christ, living a life of positive personal relational change. I am not the first to call for such a "restoration of the concept of sin to the Church."[13] The word "sin" is just one word among several that embrace concepts we need to rediscover.

Recovering a Lost Language

Helping people toward a therapeutic knowing of Christ, seeing Christ formed in them, is one of the distinctives of the journey we are outlining. But behind the journey idea is the importance of the language used, for language is one of the ways through which identity is formed.[14] Sadly, as Church and society have become more psychologically informed, they have lost some of the pastoral terms traditionally used to describe human nature and its condition. We are told that the use of such "old-fashioned" language is offensive to contemporary people. This has not been our experience.

The use of the word "sin" is a way of "being more real" in a contemporary sense. Our admission of having sin in our lives gives us a strong motivation to act. Confessing our unwillingness to change can help to give us a framework for the conflict we may so often feel. Other words also fall into this same fault line – words such as avarice, pride, idolatry, hate, contrition, repentance, suffering, sacrifice, arrogance, and eternal hope.[15] Each word is pregnant with a rich Christian tradition and its own mature theology. Such words also carry a view of human nature essential to our understanding of a Christ-likeness journey. These words can offer hope of healing wholeness change for anyone who wishes to learn their meanings from God's perspective.

Psychology has replaced many of these words with something rather different. Pride or arrogance is recognized as a self-serving bias.[16] This suggests that we all have a slight flaw in our characters, but it certainly doesn't precipitate a hunger to pursue personal positive change. It recognizes pride as a problem, even in the youngest of us, but it does not see it as *sin*, the way God describes it (Prov. 8:13).[17] Another example is unrighteous hate, which in psychology is considered a pathology.[18] Neither of these is considered a "root" or primary drive of disorder in us. They are not seen as sources of sin and rebellion against God. Instead, psychology often sees them merely as symptoms (DSM).[19]

In contrast, in pastoral care such qualities, often described emotively, are attributive primary *drives* that fragment our lives and can poison our whole nature if they are not removed by Christ (Tit. 1:15). By "drives" we mean those energies or underlying pathologies that are part of our nature, but are largely hidden to us. In Pauline theology they form part of the core of our human nature so that "what I want to do, I do not do, but what I hate I do" (Rom. 7:15). Paul speaks in plain language about his own sinful nature: its reality brought into focus by the use of straightforward words. Psychology is often in danger of softening this stark darkness and deviance in our nature.

Sin blinds our judgement, thereby permitting us arrogantly to refuse to change. These hidden contrary drives are in part woven into the fabric of our nature, even into our spirit (Gal. 5:17; 2 Cor. 4:16). A traditional psychologically-driven approach, however, will not confront such disorder in the direct way Christ does (Jn. 5:14;

8:34, etc.). Diluting the language that exposes sin helps us to excuse our refusal to change.

One of the areas of greatest distinctiveness that I have noted over the years between a Biblical and a non-Christian psychological approach to human nature is in the moral realm. For example, Scripture talks of human damage through sin, and our inability without Christ to restore ourselves. Modern psychology, however, examines us not as God sees us, but as others or we ourselves see us. Sin has therefore been largely replaced by pathology, forgiveness by insight, grace by unconditional acceptance, sanctification by growth, and holiness and its wholeness by healing.[20] Psychological therapies see sickness in some of us, whereas God sees spiritual disease in all of us. God's perspective requires everyone to focus either on Christ's view of our disorders, or on the continuing presence of spiritual disease as sin against us.

In Summary

Götz suggests that all material reality is static, while spiritual reality is in a permanent state of change.[21] God dwells mainly in this spiritual realm that is a forever changing reality. For us to harmonize with Him, therefore, we must also be willing to move personally into change through engaging spiritual reality. To *be* is to resist change. *Becoming* is a personal spiritual posture of permanent maturing change. Therefore, not seeking to change, not seeking to be like Christ, is, from God's perspective, sin. Christ's expectation was of substantial change from all His followers (Mt. 18:3). That applies to us, and will be true of us, if we welcome it.

In this chapter we have looked at the Hebrew view of sin, suggesting that it can be seen as unwillingness to change. We are not speaking here of changes in programs, structures, leadership, etc., we are not proposing that a Church that resists such change is in a place of sin, but we are saying that from the perspective of Scripture, people unwilling to seek this change are out of harmony with what God wants for them. We have also looked at the contrast between such sin and wholeness, and have considered the need to recover a lost language within the Church. The expectation of the Christian life should be toward permanent personal positive change. We all need to change both to be like Christ, and to develop greater capacity for relationality. In the next chapter we will look more closely at how this sin expresses itself in our own lives.

Notes

[1] C.W. Kiefer, *The Mantle of Maturity: A history of ideas about character development* (New York: State University of New York Press, 1988), 35.

[2] P.D. Woodbridge, "Repentance" in D.J. Atkinson and D.H. Field (eds.), *New Dictionary of Christian Ethics and Pastoral Theology* (Leicester: Inter-Varsity Press, 1995), 730–31.

[3] B. Haring, *Sin in the Secular Age* (Slough: St Paul Publications, 1974).

[4] T. Boman, *Hebrew Thought Compared to Greek* (London: SCM Press, 1954/1960), 27ff.

[5] A. McFadyen, *Bound to Sin: Abuse, holocaust and the Christian doctrine of sin* (Cambridge: Cambridge University Press, 2000), 220.

[6] A.H. Strong, *Systematic Theology: Three volumes in one* (London: Pickering & Inglis, 1907/1962), 549.

[7] J.Y. Lee, *The Theology of Change: A Christian concept of God in an Eastern perspective* (Maryknoll, N.Y.: Orbis Books, 1979), 93.

[8] See T. Wiley, *Original Sin: Origins, developments, contemporary meanings* (New York: Paulist Press, 2002).

[9] D.F. Ford, *Self and Salvation: Being transformed* (Cambridge: Cambridge University Press, 1999), 1.

[10] J.A.T. Robinson, *On Being the Church in the World* (London: SCM Press, 1960), 121ff.

[11] R. Lambourne, *Explorations in Health and Salvation* (Birmingham: Birmingham Institute for the Study of Worship and Religious Architecture, 1983), 98ff.

[12] Lee, *Theology*, 123.

[13] K. Menninger, *Whatever Happened to Sin?* (New York: Bantam Books, 1988).

[14] J.T. Wood, *Spinning the Symbolic Web: Human communication as symbolic interaction* (New Jersey: Ablex Publishing, 1992).

[15] Erikson, *Identity: Youth and crisis.*

[16] H. Gleitman, *Psychology* (New York: W.W. Norton, 1995), 436ff.

[17] L. Festinger and J.M. Carlsmith, "Cognitive consequences of forced compliance," *Journal of Abnormal and Social Psychology* 58 (1959), 203–10; E. Aronson and J.M. Carlsmith, "The effect of severity of threat on

the devaluation of forbidden behavior," *Journal of Abnormal and Social Psychology* 66 (1963), 584–8.

[18] Gleitman, *Psychology*, 758.

[19] M.B. First, *Diagnostic and Statistical Manual of Mental Disorders* (Washington: American Psychiatric Association, 1995).

[20] R. Barnes, "Psychology and spirituality: Meeting at the boundaries," *The Way Supplement* 69 (1990), 29–42; D. Benner, *Care of Souls: Revisioning Christian nurture and counsel* (Grand Rapids: Baker Books, 1998), 221.

[21] I.L. Götz, "On spirituality and teaching," *Philosophy of Education* (1997, online). Available from <www.ed.uiuc.edu/EPS/PES-Yearbook/97_docs/gotz.html> (accessed 13 January 2003).

Qualities of Christ-Likeness: Our Intellectual Life

Not all of us have had the opportunity to develop our intellectual ability. But all of us have an intellect and have views and opinions about a wide variety of subjects. The group of qualities we are now considering relate to our view of learning, and what we regard as important. Christ was a carpenter, and was also well versed in the Torah. He held no fear of those who thought they knew more than He did and engaged freely in discussion and debate. Regardless of our educational background, we have a responsibility to seek Christ-likeness in this area of our lives. In contrast to spirituality, becoming more Christ-like in our intellectual life, where the focus is on ideas rather than relationships, may initially come more easily to men than to women. But it needs to be sought by us all.

A teachable spirit

Having a teachable spirit and an intellect open to learning change is Christ-like. As John Wimber once said, this is not an age to claim to be a know-it-all. You have discovered that Christ-likeness means you see things differently from the way one normally would. You have learned to see both spiritual and material reality from God's perspective and are committed to being teachable. This is Christ-likeness.

Achieving your intellectual potential

You value intellectual understanding in yourself and others, but without despising those who have not developed this capacity. You want to fulfill your own potential without fear and are happy to explore new areas. You have become familiar with your natural skill set and are able to excel in certain areas. This is Christ-likeness.

Not afraid of being wrong

You view knowledge as a scaffold, growing in size, rather than a complete system. You know that your life will be full of learning and are comfortable changing your views as you mature. You are able to laugh at yourself when you mispronounce a word, or have your ignorance exposed. You do not mind admitting you were wrong. This is Christ-likeness.

Open to new ideas

You are able to admit that you have heard a new idea. You do not pretend that you already knew it. You are stimulated by the unfamiliar, and enjoy the company of people with more expertise than you; you can be with them without feeling intimidated. You have the capacity to hear new ideas from the Lord, noticing their resonance with your spirit, even if you do not yet know why. This is Christ-likeness.

Knowing the fundamentals and confessional Christianity

You love Scripture and are familiar with it. You know your faith and can speak about it. When you have had the opportunity, you have learned a little about the

Early Church, the creeds and the councils. You value the historical expressions of church life while also anticipating the new. This is Christ-likeness.

Never dogmatic

You are clear and confident about the fundamentals of the faith and Scripture, but you are not dogmatic about ideas. You do not need to impose your views on others. You appreciate dialogue and are able to listen to other views without necessarily having to defend your own. You are able to offer an alternative perspective without laboring the point. You don't mind if others only realize later the truth of what you said and then conclude it was their idea. This is Christ-likeness.

A love of literature, learning and the arts

You have moved beyond a narrow view of what God and human beings should be about to see Him in all forms of goodness and beauty. You take the opportunity when possible to appreciate new expressions of beauty, for example, art, literature, music, architecture and film. This is Christ-likeness.

9

The Darkness in All of Us

Before the Church can offer an appropriate language to help us in our journey of Christ-likeness, it must first be clear about its view of human nature. For our view of ourselves determines our attitude to ourselves and others. Likewise, our sense of how responsible we are for our condition determines how we feel about remedying it, and whether applying that remedy is our own or another's responsibility. Our view of our own nature will also guide our view of who God is. If we see ourselves as good-looking and talented, we are more likely to see God as benevolent. If we see ourselves as dark and evil, we may well see God (and everyone else) as malevolent.

The question of how to view human nature is far more complex than might at first appear. Unless the Church gets the foundation of human personhood right, we will be hindered in developing the idea that we all need to do a journey toward Christ-likeness. In this book we have adopted a Hebrew model of "body–spirit unity" as the foundation of our perspective of human nature. But there is another strategic contribution the Church can offer once it begins to recover its lost language. This focuses on the questions: Is human nature mostly good, or basically evil at its core? What difference can we expect Christ-likeness to make?

So What about Human Nature?

Within the Church today there is little consensus on the condition of human nature. On the one hand we have the Reformed position of "total depravity," meaning that all areas of our human nature are contaminated by the disease called sin. At the other extreme, we have the "new man" theology of modern Pentecostalism, which argues that once we are "in Christ" our old life is gone and we are a "new creation." From this triumphalist perspective, when we are sick, it is often assumed that we are either lacking faith to remove the sickness, or are not yet "converted." A contemporary Bible-based theology of human nature that takes into account both ends of the spectrum has still to be written.

In this book we have adopted a middle ground that accepts that we are both a new creation (potentially, at least!) because of what God has done, and also are all damaged by sin. A journey of growing Christ-likeness helps to ensure we can make what God has done more of a daily reality in our lives.

Lee notes that in Hebraic thought evil happens when we choose to live in disharmony with the processes of change in our lives.[1] Adam and Eve were the first to embrace this disharmony by wanting to know about evil (the fruit of the tree of the knowledge of good and evil) rather than continuing to walk with God in the garden. Human experience ever since has made the same choice, endorsing this independence from our Creator. There is now a gravity in all of us, a downward pull away from God that negatively exploits and promotes our disorders, while also being beyond them in some aspects of its powers. This we describe as Evil, or evil.

We all have this dark side to our nature. It is described in Scripture as evil (Gen. 3:1–4; Jer. 2:10–13; 17:1,9–10). Duck suggests that little serious research has been done on this subject, especially with reference to the dark side of relationships.[2] He comments, "Despite their frequency in social life, there is no deep understanding of flirtation, forgiveness, regret, remorse, disappointment, polite refusals, impolite requests, or 'needing' and bullying."[3] We all have this darkness in us, an evil mirrored in our nature.[4]

The reality of the presence of this dark side, what Jung called "the shadow,"[5] needs to be at the core of any Christ-likeness model of human make-up. The reason is not hard to find – it allows us to acknowledge that there is much in our own nature, including much that we may not yet know about, that could be working against our own best interests (Gen. 6:5; 8:21; Rom. 7:14–20, etc.)

Such a view of human nature is in marked contrast to person-centered psychological therapy (typical of modern psychologies), which seeks good in all of us, while normally not acknowledging either darkness or its sin in us. Humanism, along with other cultural ideologies, is always in danger of giving us an unrealistically optimistic view of ourselves. Likewise, some modern therapies allow us to believe that we are fundamentally good, although maybe in need of a slight tune-up. Without the language or the concept of our gravity toward the dark side of our nature, psychological therapies will struggle to expose our darkness and its self-deceit. When they ignore the concept of evil and its darkness in every one of us, they leave us with all the carnage of evil, but stripped of the tools that can help us diagnose and reconstruct our own and other peoples' broken, damaged lives.

God's perspective is clear. All He has created is good. He is the source and essence of goodness. The person He has created each of us to be is also full of that goodness, with His gift of salvation restoring this goodness in us in Christ. But we are also deeply impacted by sin and its evil. It has become part of our (fallen) nature. So when God speaks to us about ourselves during our journey into greater Christ-likeness, it will be both sides of our nature that He will want to expose, the darkness in us, and the goodness He has given us. We will discover more of who we are in Christ, with Christ formed in us, but also more of the darkness in us that must be removed through much kneading!

A Tendency toward Self-Deception

It should come as no surprise that, without a language with which to speak of sin, and without an understanding of the darkness that God sees in all of us, most of us have been handicapped on our journey into Christ-likeness. If redeemed human nature is good, what need is there for a Christ-like journey? By definition, a journey takes you from a starting point to a destination. Many of us have lived under the impression that the journey ended on the day we became a Christian, whereas from God's perspective, every day is a new opportunity for exploration and growth, for possessing more of Christ in us.

We all need to become more honest about this darkness in our relationship with God, and with others in the Church. Via has concluded – as we have in our ministry – that human nature is in a permanent place of self-deception. Most of us conceal the real narrative about ourselves with a "cover story" that we seek to promote while only half believing it.[6] Via uses the writings of Matthew and Paul in the New Testament to demonstrate that there is more than one way to be self-deceived.[7]

Some of us, in the blind arrogance of our nature, outwardly think more highly of ourselves than we should (Rom. 12:3), while denying the true darkness in us. We strive to maintain a facade, sometimes consciously, sometimes unwittingly. For others, the self-deception has the opposite impact. We live in profound self-hate and fear, resisting any attempt by others to speak well of us. Often we are a complex combination of both!

Paradoxically, it is a relief to most of us to be able to admit to ourselves that the dark side of our nature does exist. When we realize that God knows it is there and doesn't condemn us for it, we are released from the pressure of secret shame and guilt. We no longer have to pretend to be living fully successful Christian lives. We don't have to maintain our "Christian smile" or "godly" stature. We can sit down with others from the Body of Christ and, following Wesley's pattern, speak honestly of our failings, our sin, our damage. This gives so much more room for God to step in with forgiveness, grace and ongoing sanctification.

The apostle Paul recognized that we all have this dark side to our natures,[8] stating that we all need to change positively in ways that expose our own hidden/unconscious self, its sin(s) and disorder (1 Cor. 14:33; cf. Jas. 3:16). Our lifestyle of self-deceit is a violation of the authentic humanness intended for us by God. Paul notes that part of our own nature resists our becoming more like Christ or more fully human. This combination of our self-deceit, gravity toward the darkness within us, and our chosen ignorance of our true nature means that much of the time we are more likely to harm ourselves, making wrong decisions and taking wrong actions, than to do ourselves good. So how does this baggage and sin exist and operate in us?

Naming Our Baggage

The obstacles on our journey toward Christ-likeness, as well as those things that comprise the dark side of our natures, can all be specifically identified. But admitting this side of our natures is something most of us resist, for obvious reasons. While the damage remains vague it is far easier to deny our responsibility to do something about it. Yet in a journey toward greater Christ-likeness and wholeness, this darkness must be exposed so that we can face up to this responsibility. Such sin and its baggage are part of our lives in three distinct ways. So let us look at where this damage comes from:

- *Our inherited sin or baggage.* This is mostly unknown to us, but all of us inherit bad as well as good from our parents. Scripture teaches us that although none of us will be held responsible for the actual sin of our forbears, we do all suffer the consequence of their sinful actions. In Hebrew times God spoke of "four generations," suggesting that in the extended families of the Israel community, all generations living under the same roof suffer when one person sins (Ex. 20:4–5; 34:6–7; Lam. 5:7).[9] There are often patterns of broken marriages, damage to children, fighting among parents, lifestyle compulsions (e.g. smoking, alcohol, street drugs, casual sex, etc.), or giving too much time or money to congregational life while ignoring the family. These are just some of the unhelpful ways of life that we pass on to our children.

- *Sin accumulated from other people and the daily events of our lives.* We all get hurt by both relationships and circumstances. Time moves on and we may forget, but the damage stays within us. Some of this damage was intentional, inflicted on us by people who abused, betrayed or neglected us. Other baggage was accidental: the over-worked teacher who ignored us when we were bullied, or someone we loved dying prematurely and sending us into deep shock and trauma. Children are often unaware of much of this. Only in time does it become obvious. This is the area that is most commonly addressed in counseling and pastoral care. God promises to help us see this.

- *Sin we have done ourselves,* often in an attempt to prevent more damage occurring. Much of it we have either forgotten about or did not realize that it was either baggage or sin. Such damage will stand in the way of our becoming more like Christ, because much sin favors our harming ourselves. Few of us will have dealt with such deep issues at conversion because we will have been unaware of this sin and baggage. But God promises to talk about it to us if we press hard after it (1 Chr. 28:9; Is. 59:1–2; Ezek. 18:19–20; Gal. 6:7, etc.). Some of what we have harmed ourselves with will be in the form of words and curses (Ps. 42:10; Mt. 10:26–27; 26:69–75; Col. 3:9; Jas. 3:1–12). All must be found and given to Christ.

What Baggage and Sin Have I Got?

One of the biggest shocks in our growing relationship with God comes as we begin to see our own sin. But this is an essential step in the journey to greater Christ-likeness. So to help you, here is a list of a few of the areas that the Lord may want to talk to you about. We often suggest that people look through the list and mark those areas that they feel apply to them, even if only slightly. Do not be intimidated if you note a number. It is better to be honest with the Lord than to perpetuate self-deceit. Go through the list and write up your "Top Ten." In the next chapter we will begin to show you how to undo the damage with the Lord.

Areas of baggage and sin

abandonment	bitterness	covetousness
abuse	broken trust	criticism
abuse of authority	bulimia/obesity	cynicism
addictions	condemnation	despair
anorexia	confusion	deceit
arrogance	control	denial
betrayal	conceit	disappointment

disillusionment
dissociation
distrust
escapism
failure
false guilt
false selves
fear of the future
forgetfulness
frustration
greed
false grieving
grief for lost years
historic emotional
pain
hypocrisy
idealism
idolatry
impatience
isolation
judging
laziness
legalism
being let down by
others

lies
loneliness
loss
lust
manipulation
mockery
need for acceptance
negativity
obsessions
occult
paranoia
playing God
peer group slavery
perfection
piety/false religion
procrastination
rebellion
rejection
revenge
sarcasm
self-curses
self-hate
self-pity
self-sufficiency
sexual sin/impurity

shame
slavery
spiritual abuse
spiritual deceit
stress/worry
stubbornness
suicide/death
feelings
unbelief
unforgiveness
unfulfilled
expectations
unrealistic
expectations
unrighteous anger
unrighteous fear
unrighteous hate
unrighteous humor
unrighteous
jealousy
unrighteous love
unrighteous pride
vanity

My personal top ten

1

2

3

4

5

6

7

8

9

10

In Summary

Numerous authors have noted these ideas. Lapierre sees six factors or dimensions that help us experience life as a spiritual person: the journey, transcendence, community, religion, "the mystery of creation" and transformation. He describes evil as a lack of progress and/or regression in any of these six dimensions.[10] Davis puts it in a slightly different way by suggesting that Satan is a symbol of what we disown in ourselves,[11] while Ling points out that Satan ultimately derives his power from us because of our chosen ignorance.[12] These authors are all suggesting that Christ cannot take and set us free from those areas we do not own in our lives.

Part of the "good news" of the gospel is that we are all sinners, that we all have a dark side, and are all prone toward self-hurt and harm. In some of us this will not be obvious as we cover it with good works and a "spiritual" lifestyle. For others it will all already be on the surface, so we are more willing to admit and deal with it. But the darkness is in all of us, it is part of our lives, and the sooner we see it and begin a journey of dealing with it, the better it will be for us, for others and for the process of Christ being formed in us.

Notes

[1] Lee, *Theology*, 63.
[2] S.W. Duck, *Human Relationships* (London: Sage, 1986/1998), 212; W.R. Cupach and B.H. Spitzberg, *The Dark Side of Interpersonal Communication* (New Jersey: Erlbaum, 1994).
[3] Duck, *Relationships*, 212.
[4] N.G. Wright, *A Theology of the Dark Side: Putting the power of evil in its place* (Milton Keynes: Paternoster, 2003); S.J. Duffy, "Evil" in M. Downey (ed.), *The New Dictionary of Catholic Spirituality* (Collegeville, Minn.: Liturgical Press, 1993), 361–4; A. Ross, *Evangelicals in Exile: Wrestling with theology and the unconscious* (London: Darton, Longman & Todd, 1997), 103.
[5] Duck, *Relationships*, 105.
[6] D.O. Via, *Self-Deception and Wholeness in Paul and Matthew* (Philadelphia: Fortress Press, 1990), 32. But Via does not take the idea of wholeness far enough, because salvation for him, as for so many, remains a personal, private experience with no corporate dimension.

7 Via, *Self-Deception*, 137.

8 T.A. Greene, "Persona and shadow: A Jungian view of human duality" in R.L. Moore (ed.), *Carl Jung and Christian Spirituality* (New York: Paulist Press, 1988), 167–80.

9 Holmes, *More Human*, 177.

10 L.L. Lapierre, "A model for describing spirituality," *Journal of Religion and Health* 33 (1994), 2:153–61.

11 C. Davis, *Body as Spirit* (London: Hodder & Stoughton, 1976), 118.

12 T. Ling, *The Significance of Satan: New Testament demonology and its contemporary relevance* (London: SPCK, 1961), 83.

Qualities of Christ-Likeness: Family and Home

For the next group of qualities of Christ-likeness that we have compiled, we look again at relationships, this time within family and home. These are the relationships that have the highest levels of intimacy, and therefore it is here that we are most vulnerable. These are often the areas where Christ-likeness is least apparent. When we relax, the baggage seeps out! Sadly, it is those who we love, and therefore trust the most, who we also often hurt the most. The journey of Christ-likeness in this area of our lives will bring fruit not only for us, but also for our partners, our children and members of our wider family.

You might assume that most of these qualities would be easier for women than for men. But that is too simplistic. Some are about finding a healthy balance – for example, in valuing being single or married, giving and receiving love, and prioritizing family life while also being part of the Body of Christ. Women may more typically value the relationship, men more typically the task orientation, but Christ-likeness can be found in both. Christ-likeness is living the way God created us to live.

Valuing family life

> Whether single or married, you value family life and recognize it as one of the most challenging ways of life we can face today. As anyone knows, the bonuses of being married are huge, in terms both of health and

well-being. But when marriage turns sour, it can kill. You have learned to value it, even when it is not easy. If married, you do not yearn to be single. If you are single, either by choice or necessity, you do not carry an unrighteous jealousy against those who are married. You can enjoy being a parent for a season, knowing that children are a gift from the Lord. This is Christ-likeness.

Knowing that your relationship with Christ is your first commitment, you also value commitment to family life and know how to give it a righteous priority. You are living with a mature balance in the use of time, with your own and other people's families, so partners and children are honored, as are other members of the Body of Christ. You are able to do this flexibly, supporting other family members in their choices, while also knowing who can most helpfully do what. This is Christ-likeness.

Not fearing intimacy

Maturing is not just an intellectual process, but is much deeper. In your relationship with Christ, you have been known by Him in unique ways. So you carry no fear of others also knowing you deeply. Your vulnerable self has been thoroughly worked over with Him. He is the One you know intimately. Therefore, you let others know you, for Christ is part of anything you do with them, whether they know it or not. You know about human need, the importance of a hug, a touch of a hand or even eye-to-eye contact. Intimacy is something you can welcome without fear. This is Christ-likeness.

Able to give and receive love

You have learned what love is and know it is not about sexual appetite. It is not even intimacy. It is the capacity to meet everyone where they are, without judging them, while wanting Christ for them. You put others first, but without slavery to them. You have relationships where others are able to put you first and you receive their love. You know the difference between the giving and receiving of love, and the giving and receiving of a selfish self. In all this you are aware that you are engaging with God's Love and preparing for an eternity of Love. This is Christ-likeness.

Able to enjoy being single

You know that marriage is not for everyone and that most people have times of being single. This does not carry shame or stigma for you. Being single can give greater opportunity to be single-minded for the Lord. You have found the capacity to enjoy being single, and to value it in others. When we can enjoy being single, we are better qualified to be in relationship. With Him we can do both. This is Christ-likeness.

Chosen faithfulness in marriage

You value faithfulness in marriage and if married have made a decision to remain married for as long as you are able. When the relationship is difficult, you know how to stand with Christ and to love righteously anyway. You can let go of mistakes and pain without bitterness. You know how to ensure you are honored, as well as honoring your partner, and how to maintain the balance. Love is unconditional, though without slavery. This is Christ-likeness.

Openness in the home

In your relationships with those who you love, given to you for special care, you are open, even when you do not need to be. You are wise about the timing, knowing wise timing. You speak openly. You tell the truth, admitting problems. You do this in grace and love. You are able to welcome visitors to your home in openness. Your home is a safe place for family, friends and those in need. This is Christ-likeness.

Living in a "no blame" culture

You have learned enough about yourself, and those the Lord has given to you, never to allow a blame culture to emerge. Blame is never the answer. Justice, grace and mercy are. Life in the family is not about who did what. Once something has happened, you have learned to let it go and begin again. You are resolved never to allow a stalemate, the kind of deadlock where each retreats to their corner and comes out fighting for their rights. Instead, you are able to say sorry and find a constructive resolution without apportioning blame. This is Christ-likeness.

A Journey toward Christ-Likeness: How It Might Work for You

In this chapter we are going to focus on how "more of Christ" actually works. To help unpack this, we will discuss three simple ideas. First, we will introduce the idea that our human spirit can be likened to our spiritual house. This idea can help us to visualize what this journey could mean for us. Secondly, we will be taking a practical look at our emotional life to see how a change of attitude toward our feelings can help us enrich our relationship with Christ. Then, finally, we will be looking at a simple diagram that will help us understand what we can actually achieve on this journey as issue by issue we work through the obstacles standing in the path of our becoming more like Christ.

Our Spiritual House

In Chapter 7 we looked at the idea of spiritual reality, acknowledging that God created us as a body–spirit unity. Our spiritual nature is a fundamental part of our whole being. So how does our spirit look? How can we think about it in a helpful way?

Let us liken our inner spiritual life to a large run-down house. In numerous places, Scripture suggests the idea of a house (Ps. 127:1; Mt. 7:7–8; 12:44; Mk. 3:25; Lk. 11:24–26; Acts 7:49; 2 Tim. 2:20–21; Heb. 3:6, etc.). In a sense, at conversion we let God into the hallway of this spiritual house; the social Trinity enters with us. But the house is on several levels with many rooms: a basement, ground, first and second floors, and even a loft converted into rooms. Standing in the hall, the first problem we face is that every door is locked. To enter any room from the hallways, we need the key to that room.

But the problems get worse. All the rooms are full of things, both useful items and junk. We have some beautiful pieces of furniture but they are swamped by the trash. Moreover, every window of the house is open, and inevitably the rooms have been vandalized over the years by intruders climbing in at will through the windows. Until Christ entered the house we were unable to put a stop to this damage. This is because we need His help to enter the rooms and close the windows. Our Lord invites our cooperation. Together we will open all the doors, clean the rooms and close all the windows. This will stop intruders ruining our house.

But the problem is even more complicated because we no longer have any of the keys to the rooms. They were all lost long ago. Some we even threw away, promising ourselves that we would never go back there again. So before we can enter the rooms and close the windows, we need the Lord's help to find the keys. Over the door of each room there's a name or word, such as "womanhood" or "manhood," "father," "mother," "gifting", "car accident," "abuse," "anger," etc. We enter a room with the key for that room. We enter with Christ, allowing Him to redeem the room with us. We can now clean the room, keeping what we want of its contents to take into our future, and throwing out the rest. In moving into the rooms we succeed in recovering what was previously lost to us and the Lord. With open doors, the cleaned rooms – these areas of our lives – now occupied by Christ, are accessible to us, the Lord and others.

The final problem to overcome is that a number of adjoining rooms have internal doors, so it is possible to move freely from one room to another without going into the hall, and vandals can walk unchallenged between many of the rooms. When we enter the rooms, we are able to close these doors.

This illustration helps to make the important point that on our journey with Christ, we need to occupy the house fully, and begin to enjoy living in it.

Taking Possession of our House: A Meditation

We are going to imagine that you want to embark on (or continue) a journey toward greater Christ-likeness. We will assume
that you have accepted that this involves undoing areas of damage
from your history, taking personal responsibility for changing
in ways that Christ invites. You want to enjoy greater salvation
in your daily life, and live in increasing holiness and wholeness.

Here is a meditation, based on the idea of the spiritual house,
which you might find helpful as you begin to let the Lord teach
you how to take the next steps on your journey. You are unique,
so you will need to be flexible in the way you use this meditation.
It is only intended to help you get started. Read it slowly. Stop
at as many points as you wish to let the Lord talk to you, about
you. You will need to do this journey with your feelings – we
will explain why in the next section. Some people do not find
meditations helpful. So feel free to skip this or, if you prefer, just
read through it quickly.

> Imagine your spiritual house. It was originally created
> by God but over the years has had a lot of wear and tear.
> You have invited Father, Son, and Holy Spirit to take
> their rightful place in your house. They have crossed
> the threshold and begun making their home with you.
> Your growing desire is for a greater measure of God's
> presence to fill every room, making your house as it was
> originally designed to be.

> Today you are going to approach a specific room. Which
> will it be? What door has the Lord led you to? What is
> the name over the door? It may be a person, a memory, a
> feeling, an area of sin, an event, or something else. Take
> time to let all the feelings associated with the name come
> to the surface.

Jesus is with you at the door of the room. He is encouraging you to open it when you feel ready. If getting into the room feels difficult, then ask the Lord to give you a key to help you. He may do it straight away. Or it may be that the key will come in several days' time.

When you are ready to go in, the Lord will go in with you. He already knows what you will find. He comes with His light, His forgiveness, His mercy and Love, His truth, His authority as Son of God. It is His intention to bring redemption and restoration to this area of your life so that this room can contribute to the growing wholeness of your life.

What do you find as you go into the room? A feeling, a word? What do you see? Are there many things in the room? Or perhaps it is empty? Is there a draught blowing in from the open windows? Perhaps to start with you can't see anything. Take time to listen to the Lord talking to you about the room. Admit what you are thinking and feeling, preferably to someone else. You will probably discover that you already know a great deal about the room and the damage that it contains, but you are now willing to own or accept what you are thinking or feeling.

It is God's intention to help you to clean up the room. This means He wants you to give to Him each area of damage that doesn't belong there. Perhaps it is an anger you have held on to for years, or the pain of a deep loss? Is it something you are ashamed of, or a word that someone said that has hurt you deeply? God is not in a hurry. He wants to do this job thoroughly so that you can know more of His redemption in this area of your life.

As well as asking you to give to Him each item of baggage in the room (usually one piece at a time!), He will want to give <u>back</u> to you those things that you have missed all these years. What does He want to fill the room with? Ask Him. He is often very specific. For instance, He will enlist your help in redecorating so you can grow in this area of your life.

to GIVE
IN
RETURN.

Most of us encounter the problem of the housemaid, our intellect, when we are cleaning up these rooms. Don't allow yourself to think your way out of the room. Don't attempt to do the possessing and cleaning logically and sensibly. Remember that this is a <u>spiritual house</u> and God is doing <u>some deep redeeming</u>. Be willing to linger with Him. Expect both <u>knowledge from God</u> and <u>His supernatural intervention.</u>

Is God asking you to make some choices or repent of an area of sin related to this room? Invite Him to show you more. Let the feelings associated with the sin and the repentance be expressed freely as you welcome His forgiveness. Do you need to <u>close the window</u> to remove areas of <u>unrighteous vulnerability?</u>

When you are ready to stop, thank the Lord for what you have seen and what you and He have done. The dough is a little more kneaded today than it was yesterday. You may want to return to the room in a day or two's time to do some more work. Or you may prefer to move on to another room and then go back to this one some other time. Let the Lord lead you.

"Feeling is Healing"

It is important for our journey into Christ that we should be willing to have a better understanding of the spiritual world and our place in it. Imagining our spiritual house and the journey it offers will help us in this process. But first we must accept the fact that the baggage and sin locked away in us are often held captive by our feelings. So one of the most effective ways of entering and cleaning each room in our house is through our emotion and its feelings. If you look through the "baggage list" in the previous chapter, you will see that there is a strong emotional element to much of it.

Take a balloon, and blow it up. It expands. This is what toxic emotional experience does for us. The emotion of these bad times remains with most of us, collected and then repressed and/or denied by us. It fills the room in our spiritual house. We may deny that we have been hurt (keeping the door to the room closed), but the pain, though hidden, remains there in us. The emotion (the air in our balloon) keeps the memories alive. If you doubt this, then recall the time you had an instinctive shock when you saw a man like the one who assaulted you, or glimpsed across the car park a woman who looked like your ex-wife. The emotion began to flood you until you "took control" of it and repressed it again. Such experiences illustrate to all of us that our rooms are full of emotional balloons that need deflating.

So part of the journey of moving through your spiritual house is the need to engage and give to Christ this toxic emotion that is stored up in you and is keeping the bad memories alive. We need to deflate the balloon, giving the contents to Christ. As the balloon empties, so the memories are able to fade. This can happen to anyone as they let the emotion flood them, giving it to Christ as they do. Some find it helpful to imagine the cross in front of them and as they find their tears and painful emotion, they give it into the cross.

There are several ways of opening the rooms of our house, but a helpful place to start is to admit that our feelings are damaged. Our emotional life is like the cement that holds the bricks of our damaged pasts in place. We first get the understanding from the Lord of what is in the room (receiving the key to the door and entering). Then we repent of the sin and get in touch with the feelings. This is the cleansing. It involves both our cognitive thinking and our emotions.

In sweeping the room and closing the windows to others' abuse, we are able to stand more firmly with the Lord. The result will be that the Enemy and other people will have less capacity to harm us – they will no longer be able to prod the open wounds of our damaged emotion. When these windows are all closed, we and the Lord are able to occupy more of our house, allowing our relationship with Him to become more stable. This will also give us an increasing sense, as we possess more of ourselves emotionally, that we are growing in holiness. The toxic emotion is no longer there for us to poison ourselves with.

Human Emotion: God's Second Chance for Us

One of the more significant things about the journey outlined in this book is God's perspective on our human emotion. In few other areas are we more damaged than in our feelings. We need to move from a Greek view of emotion, where some feelings are good and others bad, to the more holistic, rounded Hebrew idea.[1] This Hebrew view sees all emotion and its bouquet of feelings as having both a good and bad side.

Such a view of emotion is always personally liberating. It does not condemn certain feelings (anger, hate, jealousy, etc.) but instead allows us to cleanse their toxic aspects while encouraging the discovery of a righteous dimension to all our feelings. When we have let go of toxic anger, we will then have a greater capacity to feel a righteous anger at injustice, as Jesus did. Likewise, when we have let go of our unrighteous "peace" and "calmness," we are able to be more deeply disturbed by our remaining sin in a righteous way, while also carrying "the peace that passes understanding."

Contemporary society places a great deal of importance on the authority of experience.[2] The twenty-first century is therefore not a time for the Church to be showing contempt for the "experience" of God that comes through the emotions. Doing so makes the Church appear even more out of touch than it already is. Christ expressed a range of emotions (Lk. 19:45ff.; Jn. 11:33,35, etc.) and speaks in emotional terms about the person and work of the Holy Spirit (Jn. 14:25–27; 16:8–11).

By adopting a Hebrew view of emotion – that all the feelings in our bouquet of feelings need to be cleansed – we are more able to be positive about our feelings. We can see them as friends, and not enemies of our faith. We must welcome our feelings as allies, part of our spiritual toolbox. Such an approach to emotion requires a complete reversal of the thinking of many Christians, who need to move away from a cerebral view in which some of our feelings, such as anger and jealousy, are condemned as untrustworthy. Instead, we need to see all emotion as an asset and God's second chance to engage and let go of our toxic pasts with all their pain. What we often forget in the Church is that none of us can learn without emotion.[3] As we grow in Christ-likeness, we will become more emotional in a positive way. But don't panic, God's view of emotion is radically different from ours, and we will learn to welcome it in our growing wholeness.

We are suggesting that the healing of our damaged feelings will happen naturally on our journey as we move from a place of seeing them as the enemy to a place where catharsis and the practice of emotionality help heal us. This makes our feelings among the greatest assets we have in Christ. Wholeness as Christ-likeness includes emotional maturity, so this emotionally-experienced dimension of Christ-likeness brings part of the authenticity that is being sought by all those whose lives are in emotional disorder. Emotion is a key issue among the contemporary unchurched. They see emotion in a more positive light than do most Christians, understanding that feelings can be refined by cathartic engaging and sharing.[4]

What Your Journey Could Look Like

To summarize this chapter, we are concluding with a diagram illustrating what happens to us in Christ as we deal with the things of our past. On this stage of our journey we are "taking ground" from our toxic pasts, the darkness within us and the Enemy. As we possess more and more rooms of our house, we begin to change in significant positive ways.

But, remember, the journey for men and women will be different. Also, as individuals we are unique, so each of us will do a unique journey based on the sin and baggage in our lives. This is why it is so important that we learn to let the Lord teach us what His perspective is – the *Rapha* principle (Ex. 15:26). He will help us move from one issue to the next by putting the subject on our agenda by talking to us, either through Scripture, circumstances, or through what others who we trust believe we should be doing

OUR JOURNEY TOWARD WHOLENESS:

From our false self to our person in Christ

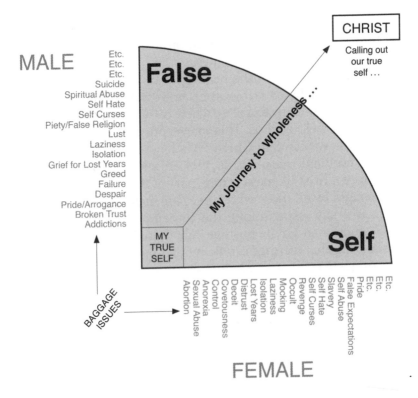

MY FALSE SELF = Who I want others to think I am!

What the diagram shows is that we all have issues in our lives that Christ wants to help us through. This is the journey toward greater Christ-likeness. It is our becoming more the person God created us to be rather than merely remaining the person we now are. Christ calls all of us out of our dark and difficult pasts, just as He called John Bunyan's pilgrim.[5] The more we possess of who we should be, giving our pasts to Christ, the more we will be able to enjoy the qualities of life that we all so dearly want.[6]

In this diagram we have used the concept of true and false selves. Over many years we have found this diagram helpful in distinguishing those areas of our lives that are authentic and therefore able to relate to God (the true self), and those areas where we are living in sin or deceit and from God's perspective are not real (the false self). Our Christ-like journey is our being willing to see the areas of sin and baggage and then move into reality by identifying and repenting of them before Christ, changing both our values and lifestyle. As we do this, we are welcoming more of our true self into each room of our spiritual house, while letting go of our false self and its accompanying darkness. This involves the need for us to change our lifestyles and begin to practice a range of new habits.

In Summary

This chapter describes some of the practicalities of undoing all that stands in the way of our growing Christ-likeness. A Christianity that leaves us unchanged, with our lives no different from those around us who do not confess Christ, is not an authentic faith. To varying degrees, we all need to change our behavior, beginning to make decisions that are good for us and honor both Christ and others. But changing our behavior, acknowledging the underlying darkness and its emotion, will often lead only to conflict and turmoil. Practicing and living our growing in Christ-likeness will need a number of honest moments and clear decisions, first to face the darkness in us, and then to give it to Christ, so that we can radically change the way that we live and prioritize or lives.

Throughout this book we have been noting numerous positive characteristics that will become evident in our lives as and when we are willing to learn new ways of living with and for Christ. For all of us, discipleship should be about what Christ-likeness is and how we can welcome it in a practical way. A life committed to Christ that is little different from our previous lifestyle will not get the commendation from the Lord, "Well done, good and faithful servant."

Notes

1. I would not want to be entirely either/or on this matter. For instance, Aquinas, working within this Greek philosophical framework, had some good things to say about emotion. See Thomas Aquinas, *Summa theologiae. The emotions* (London: Eyre & Spottiswoode, 1967) and C.R. Hess, "Aquinas organic synthesis of Plato and Aristotle," *Angelicum* 58 (1981), 339–50.

2. Goleman, *Emotional Intelligence*; J. Diamond, *Life Energy: Using the meridians to unlock the hidden power of your emotions* (St Paul, Minn.: Paragon House, 1985/1990).

3. J. le Dioux, *The Emotional Brain: The mysterious underpinnings of emotional life* (London: Weidenfeld & Nicolson, 1998).

4. H.B. English and A.C. English, "Catharsis" in H.B. English and A.C. English (eds.), *A Comprehensive Dictionary of Psychological and Psychoanalytical Terms: A guide to usage* (London: Longman, 1958), 54.

5. J. Bunyan, *The Pilgrim's Progress* (London: Penguin, 1656/1987).

6. In volume 3 of this series of books, we will be focusing on ancient–future Church, looking at what needs to change in our churches in order for them to serve contemporary people more effectively. We will be unpacking some of the implications of social Trinity (from volume 1), and applying the model of a wholeness Christ-centered journey (given in this book) to a local church context.

Qualities of Christ-Likeness:
The World

Your walk with Christ is not just about Him and you. It involves the whole world, in which God has placed you. We have seen throughout the book that Christ-likeness does not mean separation from the world. Nor does it mean simply preaching Christ to the world. Christ being formed in us will impact every area of our lives. The imaginary divide between secular and sacred disappears as we bring our Christ-centered spirituality to every activity and relationship, whatever our realms of responsibilities. For women, these qualities often express themselves in righteous curiosity and are relationally-oriented. For men, they are often more conceptual, taking in the broader landscape. There are numerous different ways of expressing these characteristics of Christ-likeness. What will yours be?

Living a healthy, inclusive lifestyle

> Your growing new values are having a profound impact on every area of your life. In Hebrew thought God adopted a land, a city and a people, and you seek to live this principle in your life. You are involved in some way in the life of the country you are part of, regardless of the politics. You are giving back. As you have opportunity, you are actively involved in your local area and community, whether urban or rural. You are giving back. Your growing love for people extends to people of any

faith and of none. You have an ability to honor all those whose lives you touch. All are part of your relationship with Christ Himself, earthing every area of your life, and all its relationships, in the significance of Christ to you, and you to Him. Your life and lifestyle are inclusive of all you are becoming in Christ. This is Christ-likeness.

Lover of the natural world

The natural world, God's creation, is an enchantment to you. You love to learn about it when you have the time. You delight in the God who could create so many different species of birds of paradise, or shades of color on an egg. The natural world tells us so much about our Creator, who would not want to know more? This is Christ-likeness.

Living an ecologically sensitive lifestyle

You are aware of your own responsibility for the world. You support efforts to stop global warming, and do not advocate policies that put one person or country above all others. You have made changes to your lifestyle because of what you have learned about being a responsible citizen, perhaps including recycling, saving electricity, fair trade, etc. You do not judge others for their lifestyles but you live out your commitment to God's creation, gently, quietly, graciously. This is Christ-likeness.

Politically and socially aware

You seek to be informed about global events and to learn more whenever possible. You have let the Lord talk to you about nations and peoples and you are able to pray into these issues. You have prayer-walked other areas of the globe from your home. This is Christ-likeness.

A citizen of this world, without compromise

You are not one of those people who are so heavenly minded that you are of no earthly use. Nor do you view this world as evil. You are able to live with Christ, seeing the world from His perspective, and you love being part of this world now. You anticipate the day when it is redeemed by Christ as a new creation. You are proud to be a citizen of this world. This is Christ-likeness.

Delighting without possessing

You do not need to own things to enjoy them. You are able to live life fully while owning very little. You are able to appreciate things for a season and then let them go. When you have the opportunity to, you can give away possessions that you treasure. You will have one eye on eternity, the other on beautiful things as you pass them, delighting in them without wanting to possess them. This is Christ-likeness.

Enjoying your citizenship

When you leave this world you will be missed in a whole range of areas, for instance, in your neighborhood, in your job, in your circle of friends, and, of course, in your family. You will be paid the very greatest compliment that one can offer any human being – that there will be less of Christ around because you have gone to be with Him. You will be missed because you were a full citizen of both worlds. This is Christ-likeness.

11

"Christ in Me?"

There is a sense in which Christ is in everything (Col. 3:11). But there is another sense in which, when we invite Him, He is in each one of us in a unique way (Col. 1:27). He is both in us, and also in the whole world around us, the material and spiritual realities. In another sense, He also covers us (Col. 3:14).

Yet many of us find it so much easier to imagine Christ walking with us than to think of Him being in us. We can envisage Him walking alongside the two disciples on the road to Emmaus. We can ask Him to be with us in difficult situations. We can welcome His presence in church meetings. But to have Christ living "in us" seems an entirely different matter.

Why is "in us" such a problem for some of us? One of the reasons could be that so many bad things have happened to us, in us, in our pasts that we cannot think of anything that is in us ever being good. Another reason may be that God being alongside us means we can walk away from Him if we want to. But if He indwells us, then in a sense we are stuck with each other.

Our resistance to this idea of Christ being in us is, of course, futile because from God's perspective it has already happened. We are new creations. We have been saved and redeemed, cleansed by His blood. We may live in denial, pretending that when we close down our awareness of His indwelling, He isn't really there, but Father, Son and Holy Spirit have already entered our house, even if only into the hallway. We can try to limit the intrusion, keep doors closed and control the consequences of His presence, but this will bring about conflict within us and only achieve modest "success."

It is better for us to embrace wholly the God-given reality of being in the family of God, His sons and daughters, with Christ in us and us in Him.

So how does Christ being in us actually work? The principle is a simple one. As the blood of Christ cleanses us, so the Holy Spirit can fill us (Rom. 8:1ff.; 1 Jn. 5:6ff.). When the Holy Spirit comes, He brings the presence of Christ. This process, as we surrender to Him, allows the Lord to indwell us and work through us. But He cannot do this alongside us: only from within us. So in effect Christ in me has three dimensions: Christ is in me for Him, Christ is in me for me, and Christ is in me for others. Without Christ being in me, I cannot ever wholly be me. Without Christ being in me, I cannot grow in Christ-likeness. Here the analogy of the dough fails us, and our being kneaded becomes a very inadequate concept. Christ is also in the dough. He kneads the dough from the inside. Yes, He did create the dough and now, in a sense, as the yeast in the dough, He will ensure that the dough rises to become a delicious loaf of hot fresh bread!

What Does "Christ in Me" Really Mean?

"Christ in me" has a whole raft of implications for me, others and Christ Himself. To begin with, it is the indwelling of Christ that gives form to our relationships with others in the Body of Christ (1 Jn. 4:11–12). It also means that we have the potential to do greater things than we can do alone. "Christ in me" becomes the hope of our lives: with Him we can do things impossible for us to do on our own.

But it is not only in our relationships with others that we can do more. With Christ in us, we ourselves are able to become more ourselves. We fulfill more of *imago Dei*. The indwelling Christ somehow takes what is ours as we progressively give it to Him, and allows our own uniqueness, given originally by Him, to shine both in and through us. But it does not end there.

One of the main ways we experience a bridging of both our natural and spiritual worlds is through the experience of spiritual gifting. As we find Christ in us, we can also begin to move in spiritual gifting and anointing. The healing in our own journeys will give us much new ground to move into – we will recover areas of our lives that previously were off limits because they were claimed by our sin, baggage and the Enemy.

One final area of understanding that we all need to grasp is that with Christ we are never alone. He is in us. We are in Him. What this means practically is that we are beginning a long journey of restoring what was lost by the first Adam (Rom. 5:12–14). This will one day be a full restoration of ourselves to God. But we will know enough of Christ in this present life to call Him Master and Friend, as well as knowing that He is closer than a brother.

What Then Is Our Task?

Essentially, our task in life is to see Christ formed in us, and then, as we do this, to help others do the same. This is the discipleship journey; this is the command of Christ. But it also involves us in other things. To begin with, we must acknowledge a direct link between what we are in Christ and who we are in relationships. If the journey each of us is making with Christ does not also give us love for others, then our life is not authentic and our journey is (to some degree) a fake (1 Jn. 4:20b).

This journey must also call out life from us toward others, and vice versa. There must be a direct correlation between who we are becoming in Christ and how this positively impacts those around us. For instance, no one should be able to look at us on a Christ-like journey and say, "If that's what happens to them, then forget it!" To be authentic, the journey and its positive outcomes must be attractive and contagious.

Also, we must be aware in ourselves that we are changing. We may not know it straightaway, but we must come to *know* that this works for us. We should never let ourselves be tempted to lie by denying the good about being a Christian. We and the Lord are the principal benefactors. This is why we do this journey, for Christ and for His Kingdom (Col. 1:24–29).

Scripture sometimes gives us glimpses into God's perspective in ways that we can easily miss. For instance, in Romans 8:18 Paul suggests, almost by a slip of the tongue, that one day we will all know what it means to have Christ in us: "I consider that our present sufferings are not worth comparing with the glory that will be revealed *in us.*" His glory in and shining out of us? This is something few of us can now imagine. But although a promise to us all, it does not take from us our task in this life to see Christ more fully formed in us. He will fully complete this task in all of us one day, when we finally stand before Him. May we be found worthy of such honor.

Bibliography

Adams, J.E., *What about Nouthetic Counseling? A question and answer book* (Grand Rapids: Baker Books, 1977)

—, *A Thirst for Wholeness: How to gain wisdom from the book of James* (Stanley, N.C,: Timeless Texts, 1988/1997)

Aden, L., "Faith and the developmental cycle," *Journal of Pastoral Psychology* 24 (1976), 3:215–30

Aden, L., et al. (eds.), *Christian Perspectives on Human Development* (Grand Rapids: Baker Books, 1992)

Allport, G.W., *Becoming: Basic considerations for a psychology of personality* (New Haven: Yale University Press, 1955)

—, *Pattern and Growth in Personality* (New York: Holt, Rinehart & Winston, 1961)

Aquinas, T., *Summa theologiae. The emotions* (London: Eyre & Spottiswoode, 1967)

Armirtham, S. and R.J. Pryor, *The Invitation to the Feast of Life: Resources for spiritual formation in theological education* (Geneva: World Council of Churches, Programme on Theological Education, 1991)

Aronson, E. and J.M. Carlsmith, "The effect of severity of threat on the devaluation of forbidden behavior," *Journal of Abnormal and Social Psychology* 66 (1963), 584–8

Ashton, M., *Growing in Wholeness* (Eastbourne: Kingsway, 1985)

Auten, N., *From Fear to Faith: Studies of suffering and wholeness* (London: SPCK, 1971)

Barnes, R., "Psychology and Spirituality: Meeting at the boundaries," *The Way Supplement* 69 (1990), 29–42

Benner, D.G., *Care of Souls: Revisioning Christian nurture and counsel* (Grand Rapids: Baker Books, 1998)

Benner, D.G. and J.H. Ellens, "Conclusion" in Aden, L., D.G. Benner and J.H. Ellens (eds.), *Christian Perspectives on Human Development* (Grand Rapids: Baker Books, 1992), 251–4

Benson, P.L., et al., "The faith-maturity scale: Conceptualization, measurement and empirical validation" in Lynn, M.L. and D.O. Moberg (eds.), *Research in the Social Scientific Study of Religion*, vol. 5 (Greenwich, Conn.: JAI Press), 1–26

Beuchner, R., "Journey toward Wholeness," *Theology Today* 49 (1993), 4:454–64

Boman, T., *Hebrew Thought Compared to Greek* (London: SCM Press, 1954/1960)

Booth, H., *Healing is Wholeness: A resource book to encourage healing ministry initiatives in the local church* (London: The Churches Council for Health and Healing, 1987)

Boyd, J.H., *Reclaiming the Soul: The search for meaning in a self-centered culture* (Cleveland, Ohio: The Pilgrim Press, 1996)

Bright, B., *Handbook for Christian Maturity* (A Compilation of Ten Basic Steps toward Christian Maturity) (Orlando, Fla.: Campus Crusade for Christ, New Life Resources, 1981)

Brown, L., *New Shorter Oxford English Dictionary*, two volumes (Oxford: Clarendon Press, 1993)

Brown, W.S. (ed.), *Whatever Happened to the Soul? Scientific and theological portraits of human nature* (Minneapolis: Augsburg Fortress, 1998)

Bunyan, J., *The Pilgrim's Progress* (London: Penguin, 1656/1987)

Burkhardt, M.A. and M.G. Nagai-Jacobson, "Reawakening spirit in clinical practice," *Journal of Holistic Nursing* 12 (1994), 1:9–21

Burnard, P., "Spiritual distress and the nursing response," *Journal of Advanced Nursing* 12 (1987), 377–82

Chriss, J.J. (ed.), *Counseling and the Therapeutic State* (New York: Aldine de Gruyter, 1999)

Clark, T.E. and M. Thompson, "Psychology and spirituality: meeting at the boundaries," *The Way Supplement* 69 (1990), 29–42

Cobb, J.B., *Theology and Pastoral Care* (Philadelphia: Fortress Press, 1977)

Collinson, S.I., *An enquiry into the congruence of discipling as an educational strategy with the objective of Christian faith communities*, PhD thesis (Murdoch University, Perth, Western Australia, 1999)

Come, A.B., *Human Spirit and Holy Spirit* (Philadelphia: The Westminster Press, 1959)

Conger, J.J., *Adolescence and Youth: Psychological development in a changing world* (New York: Harper & Row, 1973)

Conn, J.W., *Spirituality and Personal Maturity* (New York: Integration Books, 1989)

Conran, T., "Solemn Witness: A pilgrimage to Ground Zero at the World Trade Center," *Journal of Systemic Therapies* 21 (2002), 3:39–47

Covey, S.R., "Principles hold key to leadership success," *Professional Manager* 41 (September 2001), 29–30

Crabb, L., *The Safest Place on Earth: Where people connect and are forever changed* (Nashville: Word, 1999)

Cupach, W.R. and B.H. Spitzberg, *The Dark Side of Interpersonal Communication* (New Jersey: Erlbaum, 1994)

Davis, C., *Body as Spirit* (London: Hodder & Stoughton, 1976)

Davis, R. and G. Rupp (eds.), *A History of the Methodist Church in Great Britain* (London: Epworth Press, 1965)

Diamond, J., *Life Energy: Using the meridians to unlock the hidden power of your emotions* (St Paul, Minn.: Paragon House, 1985/1990)

le Dioux, J., *The Emotional Brain: The mysterious underpinnings of emotional life* (London: Weidenfeld & Nicolson, 1998)

Drakeford, D., *Integrity Therapy* (Waco, Tex.: Broadman Press, 1967)

Drane, J., *Rebuilding the Household of Faith: Being spiritual, human and Christian in today's world* (2002, online). Available from www.ctbi.org.uk/assembly/Drane.doc (accessed 29 February 2004)

Duck, S.W., *Human Relationships* (London: Sage, 1986/1998)

Duffy, S.J., "Evil" in Downey, M. (ed.), *The New Dictionary of Catholic Spirituality* (Collegeville, Minn.: Liturgical Press, 1993), 361–4

Dunlop, M.V., *Stillness and Strength and Contemplative Meditation* (Guildford: Fellowship of Meditation, 1970)

English, H.B. and A.C. English, "Catharsis" in English, H.B. and A.C. English (eds.), *A Comprehensive Dictionary of Psychological and Psychoanalytical Terms: A guide to usage* (London: Longman, 1958), 54

Erikson, E.H., *Childhood and Society* (New York: W.W. Norton, 1950/1993)

—, *Identity and the Life Cycle* (New York: W.W. Norton, 1959/1980)

—, *Identity: Youth and Crisis* (New York: W.W. Norton, 1968)

Erikson, E.H. and J.M. Erikson, *The Life Cycle Completed: A review* (New York: W.W. Norton, 1997)

Etzioni, A., *The Spirit of Community: Rights, responsibilities and the communitarian agenda* (London: Fontana Press, 1995)

Festinger, L. and J.M. Carlsmith, "Cognitive consequences of forced compliance," *Journal of Abnormal and Social Psychology* 58 (1959), 203–10

Field, A., *From Darkness to Light: How one became a Christian in the Early Church* (Ben Lomond, Calif.: Conciliar Press, 1978/1997)

Finn, T.M., *Early Christian Baptism and the Catechumenate: West and East Syria* (Minneapolis: Liturgical Press, 1992)

First, M.B., *Diagnostic and Statistical Manual of Mental Disorders* (Washington: American Psychiatric Association, 1995)

Ford, D.F., *Self and Salvation: Being transformed* (Cambridge: Cambridge University Press, 1999)

Foster, R., *Richard Foster Omnibus: "Celebration of Discipline", "Money, Sex and Power", "Prayers from the Heart"* (London: Hodder & Stoughton, 1996)

Fouch, R.E., *What is the experience of spirituality within psychotherapy? A heuristic study of seven psychotherapists' experience of spirituality within psychotherapy,* Dissertation (The Union Institution, USA, 1997)

Fowler, J.W., "Religious institutions 1: Toward a developmental perspective on faith," *Journal of Religious Education* 69 (1974), 2:207–19

—, *Stages of Faith: The psychology of human development and the quest for meaning* (San Francisco: Harper, 1981)

—, "Theology and psychology in the study of faith development" in Kepnes, S. and D. Tracy (eds.), *Concilium: Religion in the eighties* (Edinburgh: T&T Clark, 1982)

Fowler, J.W., "Pluralism and oneness in religious experience: William James, faith development theory and clinical practice" in Shafranske, E.P. (ed.), *Religion and the Clinical Practice of Psychology* (Washington: American Psychological Association, 1996), 165–86

Freud, S., *Introductory Lectures on Psychoanalysis*, vols. 15 and 16 (London: Hogarth, 1905/1965)

Frost, R., *Christ and Wholeness* (Eastbourne: Kingsway, 2000)

Fullan, M., *Change Forces: The sequel* (Philadelphia: Routledge Falmer, 1999)

Furedi, F., "The silent ascendancy of therapeutic culture in Britain," *Society* 39 (2002), 3:16–24

Gibson, T.L., "Wholeness and transcendence in the practice of pastoral psychotherapy from a Judaeo Christian perspective" in Young-Eisendrath, P. and M.E. Miller (eds.), *The Psychology of Mature Spirituality* (Philadelphia: Routledge, 2000), 175–86

Gilligan, C., *In a Different Voice* (Cambridge, Mass.: Harvard University Press, 1982/1993)

Gleitman, H., *Psychology* (New York: W.W. Norton, 1995)

Goldbrunner, J., *Holiness is Wholeness* (London: Burns & Oates, 1955)

Goleman, D., *Emotional Intelligence* (New York: Bantam Books, 1995)

—, *The New Leaders: Transforming the art of leadership into the science of results* (London: Little Brown, 2002)

—, *Social Intelligence: The new science of human relationship* (London: Hutchinson, 2006)

Götz, I.L., "On spirituality and teaching," *Philosophy of Education* (1997, online). Available from <www.ed.uiuc.edu/EPS/PES-Yearbook/97_docs/gotz.html> (accessed 13 January 2003)

Goudie, N., *Developing Spiritual Wholeness* (London: World Books/ Word, 1972/1992)

Greene, T.A., "Persona and Shadow: A Jungian view of human duality" in Moore, R.L. (ed.), *Carl Jung and Christian Spirituality* (New York: Paulist Press, 1988), 167–80

Groeschel, B.J., *Spiritual Passages: The psychology of spiritual development* (New York: Crossroad Publishing, 1992)

Gross, J., *One: Returning to Wholeness* (New York: Tabby House/ Portico Press, 2004)

Gunn, G., *Office Feng Shui* (Abingdon: Hodder & Stoughton, 1999)

Haring, B., *Sin in the Secular Age* (Slough: St Paul Publications, 1974)

—, *Christian Maturity: Holiness in today's world* (Slough: St Paul Publications, 1983)

Hay, D. and K. Hunt, *Understanding the Spirituality of People who don't go to Church* (Nottingham: Nottingham University Press, 2000)

Henderson, D.M., *John Wesley's Class Meeting: A model for making disciples* (Nappanee, Ind.: Evangel Publishing House, 1997)

Hess, C.R., "Aquinas organic synthesis of Plato and Aristotle," *Angelicum* 58 (1981), 339–50

Holmes, P.R., *Becoming More Human: Exploring the interface of spirituality, discipleship and therapeutic faith community* (Milton Keynes: Paternoster, 2005)

—, *Trinity in Human Community: Exploring congregational life in the image of the social Trinity* (Milton Keynes: Paternoster, 2006)

—, "Spirituality: some disciplinary perspectives" in Flanagan, K. and P.C. Jupp (eds.), *The Sociology of Spirituality* (Ashgate, 2007)

—, *Fasting: A Biblical handbook* (forthcoming 2008)

Holmes, P.R. and S.B. Williams, *Changed Lives: Extraordinary stories of ordinary people* (Milton Keynes: Authentic Media, 2005)

—, *Church as a Safe Place: A handbook. Confronting, resolving and minimizing abuse in the Church* (Milton Keynes: Authentic Media, 2007)

Hughes, S., *God Wants You Whole: The way to healing, health and wholeness* (Eastbourne: Kingsway, 1984)

Hurding, R., *Pathways to Wholeness: Pastoral care in a postmodern age* (London: Hodder & Stoughton, 1998)

Izzard, S., "Holding contradictions together: an object relational view of healthy spirituality," *Contact* 140 (2003), 1:2–8

Jacobs, J.M., *Toward the Fulness of Christ: Pastoral care and Christian maturity* (London: Darton, Longman & Todd, 1988)

Janov, A., *Primal Scream: Primal therapy, the cure for neurosis* (New York: Delta, 1970)

Johnson, E.L., "Whatever Happened to the Human Soul? A brief Christian genealogy of a psychological term," *Journal of Psychology and Theology, Special Issue: Perspectives on the Self/Soul* 26 (1998), 1:16–28

Jung, C.G., *Modern Man in Search of a Soul*, translated by Dell, W.S.B. and H.G. Baynes (London: Routledge, 1933/1973)

Kao, C.C.L., *Maturity and the Quest for Spiritual Meaning* (New York: University Press of America, 1988)

Keating, T., *The Spiritual Journey: A guide book with tapes* (Colorado Springs, Colo.: Contemporary Publications, 1987)

Kiefer, C.W., *The Mantle of Maturity: A history of ideas about character development* (New York: State University of New York Press, 1988)

Koenig, H.G., "Religion, spirituality and medicine: a rebuttal to skeptics," *International Journal of Psychiatry in Religion* 29 (1999), 2:123–31

Lambourne, R., *Explorations in Health and Salvation* (Birmingham: Birmingham Institute for the Study of Worship and Religious Architecture, 1983)

Lapierre, L.L., "A model for describing spirituality," *Journal of Religion and Health* 33 (1994), 2:153–61

Lee, J.Y., *The Theology of Change: A Christian concept of God in an Eastern perspective* (Maryknoll, N.Y.: Orbis Books, 1979)

Levinson, D.J., *The Seasons of a Man's Life* (New York: Ballantine Books, 1978)

Ling, T., *The Significance of Satan: New Testament demonology and its contemporary relevance* (London: SPCK, 1961)

MacMullen, R., *Christianizing the Roman Empire (AD 100–400)* (New Haven: Yale University Press, 1984)

Martin, P., *The Sickening Mind: Brain, behaviour, immunity and disease* (London: Flamingo, 1998)

Martsolf, D.S. and J.R. Mickley, "The concept of spirituality in nursing theories: differing world-views and extent of focus," *Journal of Advanced Nursing* 27 (1998), 294–303

May, R., "The problem of will, decision and responsibility in psychological health," *The Christian Scholar* 66 (1963), 3:235–44

McFadyen, A., *Bound to Sin: Abuse, holocaust and the Christian doctrine of sin* (Cambridge: Cambridge University Press, 2000)

McGrath, A.E., "Sin and salvation" in Atkinson, D.J. and D.H. Field (eds.), *New Dictionary of Christian Ethics and Pastoral Theology* (Leicester: Inter-Varsity Press, 1995), 78-87

Menninger, K., *Whatever Happened to Sin?* (New York: Bantam Books, 1988)

Merton, T., *The Ascent to Truth* (London: Hollis & Carter, 1951)

—, *The New Man* (New York: Farrar, Strauss & Giroux, 1961)

—, *Life and Holiness* (New York: Doubleday/Image Books, 1963/ 1996)

Middlemiss, D., *Interpreting Charismatic Experience* (London: SCM Press, 1996)

Mitroff, I.I. and E.A. Dentron, *A Spiritual Audit of Corporate America: A hard look at spirituality, religion and values in the workplace* (San Francisco: Jossey-Bass, 1999)

Moon, G.W., "A personal journey to spiritually sensitive psychotherapy: An interview with David G. Benner," *Journal of Psychology and Christianity* 21 (2002), 1:64–71

Nee, W., *Spiritual Authority* (New York: Christian Fellowship Publishers, 1972)

Nicholson, K., *Body and Soul: The transcendence of materialism* (Boulder, Colo.: Westview Press, 1997)

Nygren, A., *Agape and Eros* (London: SPCK, 1937; Chicago: Chicago Press, 1982)

O'Connor, T.J., "Review of quantity and types of spirituality research in three health care databases (1962–1999): implications for the health care ministry," *Journal of Pastoral Care and Counseling* 56 (2002), 3:227–32

Oden, T.C., "The historic pastoral care tradition: A resource for Christian psychologists," *Journal of Psychology and Theology* 20 (1992), 2:137–46

Offner, H., *Fruit of the Spirit: Growing in the likeness of Christ – A life-builder Bible Study* (Milton Keynes: Scripture Union, 1991)

Pease, A. and B. Pease, *The Definitive Book of Body Language* (London: Orion, 2004)

le Peau, A., *Ephesians: Wholeness for a broken world* (London: Inter-Varsity Press/SU, 2000)

Peck, M.S., *The Different Drum: Community-making and peace* (New York: Simon & Schuster, 1987)

Peterson, E.H., *The Message: The Bible in contemporary language* (Colorado Springs: Navpress, 2002)

van Peursen, C.A., *Body, Soul, Spirit: A survey of the body–mind problem*, translated by Hoskins, H.H. (London: Oxford University Press, 1966)

Philip, J., *Christian Maturity* (Leicester: Inter-Varsity Press, 1964/73)

Piaget, J., *The Language and Thought of the Child* (New York: Harcourt Brace, 1926/1956)

—, "Piaget's theory" in Mussen, P.H. (ed.), *Carmichael's Manual of Child Psychology* (New York: Wiley, 1970)

—, *The Development of Thought: Equilibration of cognitive structures* translated by Rosin, A (New York: Viking, 1977)

Popkes, W., "New Testament principles of wholeness: (and spiritual growth)," *Evangelical Quarterly* 64 (1992), 319–32

Price, C.W., *Christ For Real: How to grow in God's likeness* (Grand Rapids: Kregel Publications, 1995)

Purton, A.C., "Unconditional positive regard and its spiritual implications" in Thorne, B. and E. Lambers (eds.), *Person Centred Therapy: A European perspective* (London: Sage, 1998), 23–37

Quinn, R.E., *Deep Change: Discovering the leader within* (San Francisco: Jossey-Bass, 1996)

Rahner, K., *Nature and Grace* (London: Sheed & Ward, 1963)

—, "Mystery" in Darlap, A., et al. (eds.), *Sacramentum Mundi: An encyclopaedia of theology*, vol. 4 of 6 (London: Burns & Oates, 1978), 133–6

Regan, D., *Experience the Mystery – Pastoral possibilities for Christian mystagogy* (London: Geoffrey Chapman, 1994)

Reid, M.A., "Sanctification" in Atkinson, D.J., D.H. Field and D. Field (eds.), *New Dictionary of Christian Ethics and Pastoral Theology* (Leicester: Inter-Varsity Press, 1995), 756–7

Robb, J.H., *Man as Infinite Spirit* (Milwaukee: Marquette University Publications, 1974)

Roberts, R.C., "Virtue" in Atkinson, D.J. and D.H. Field (eds.), *New Dictionary of Christian Ethics and Pastoral Theology* (Leicester: Inter-Varsity Press, 1995), 881

Robinson, J.A.T., *On Being the Church in the World* (London: SCM Press, 1960)

Roof, W.C., *Spiritual Marketplace: Baby-boomers and the remaking of American religion* (Princeton, N.J.: Princeton University Press, 1999)

Ross, A., *Evangelicals in Exile: Wrestling with theology and the unconscious* (London: Darton, Longman & Todd, 1997)

Sanders, J.O., *In Pursuit of Maturity* (Eastbourne: Kingsway Publications, 1985)

Savage, S., S. Collins-Mayo, B. Mayo and G. Cray, *Making Sense of Generation Y: The worldview of 15–25-year-olds* (London: Church House Publishing, 2006)

Schaeffer, F.A., *True Spirituality* (London: Hodder & Stoughton, 1972)

Schermer, V.L., *Spirit and Psyche: A new paradigm for psychology, psychoanalysis and psychotherapy* (London: Jessica Kingsley, 2003)

Schippers, R., "Telos" in Brown, C. (ed.), *The New International Dictionary of New Testament Theology*, vol. 2 of 3 (Milton Keynes: Paternoster, 1971), 59–65

Schwartz, R.C., "Releasing the soul: Psychotherapy as a spiritual practice" in Walsh, F. (ed.), *Spiritual Resources in Family Therapy* (New York: Guilford Publications, 1999)

Shafranske, E.P. (ed.), *Religion and the Clinical Practice of Psychology* (Washington: American Psychological Association, 1996)

Shelton, R.L., *Divine Expectations: Interpreting the atonement for 21st century mission* (Waynesboro, Ga.: Paternoster, 2006)

Skarsaune, O., *In the Shadow of the Temple: Jewish influences on early Christianity* (Downers Grove, Ill.: Inter-Varsity Press, 2002)

Steere, D.A., *Spiritual Presence in Psychotherapy: A guide for care-givers* (New York: Brunner-Mazelle, 1997)

Strong, A.H., *Systematic Theology: Three volumes in one* (London: Pickering & Inglis, 1907/1962)

Thomas, F.A., *Spiritual Maturity: Preserving congregational health and balance* (Philadelphia: Fortress Press, 2002)

Twelftree, G., *Jesus the Exorcist: A contribution to the study of the historical Jesus* (Peabody, Mass.: Hendrickson, 1993)

Underhill, E., *The Mystics of the Church* (New York: Schocken Books, 1964)

Van Kaam, A., *Fundamental Formation* (New York: Crossroad, 1983)

Via, D.O., *Self-Deception and Wholeness in Paul and Matthew* (Philadelphia: Fortress Press, 1990)

Wade, C.R., L. Bowman and C. Bowman, *The Jesus Principle: Building churches in the image of Christ* (Arlington, Tex.: Clear Stream, 1998)

White, J., *Christ likeness* (Colorado: Navpress, 1996)

Wiersbe, W., *Be Mature: How to break the mould of spiritual immaturity, and grow up in Christ* (Wheaton, Ill.: Victor Books, 1978)

Wilber, K., "Spirituality and developmental lines: Are there stages?" *Journal of Transpersonal Psychology* 31 (1999), 1:1–10

Wiley, T., *Original Sin: Origins, developments, contemporary meanings* (New York: Paulist Press, 2002)

Wilhoit, J.C., *Nurture that is Christian: Developmental perspectives on Christian education* (Wheaton, Ill.: Victor Books, 1995)

Wilkinson, J., *The Bible and Healing: A medical and theological commentary* (Edinburgh: The Handsel Press, 1998)

Willard, D., *Divine Conspiracy* (San Francisco: Harper, 1998)

Williams, S.B. and P.R. Holmes, *Letting God Heal: From emotional illness to wholeness* (Milton Keynes: Authentic Media, 2004)

Wood, J.T., *Spinning the Symbolic Web: Human communication as symbolic interaction* (New Jersey: Ablex Publishing, 1992)

Woodbridge, P.D., "Repentance" in Atkinson, D.J. and D.H. Field (eds.), *New Dictionary of Christian Ethics and Pastoral Theology* (Leicester: Inter-Varsity Press, 1995), 730–1

Wright, N.G., *A Theology of the Dark Side: Putting the power of evil in its place* (Milton Keynes: 2003)

Young-Eisendrath, P. and M.E. Miller (eds.), *The Psychology of Mature Spirituality: Integrity, wisdom, transcendence* (London: Routledge, 2000)

Zohar, D. and I. Marshall, *SQ The ultimate intelligence: Connecting with our spiritual intelligence* (London: Bloomsbury Publishing, 2000)

Author Index

Adams, J.E. 34, 85
Aden, L. 34
Allport, G.W. 28, 33, 34, 60, 68
Aquinas, T. 48, 142
Armirtham, S. 101
Aronson, E. 114
Ashton, M. 85
Auten, N. 85

Barnes, R. 115
Benner, D.G. 28, 33, 34, 77, 115
Benson, P.L. 29, 34
Beuchner, R. 77, 86
Boman, T. 114
Booth, H. 85
Boyd, J.H. 82, 86, 101
Bright, B. 35
Brown, L. 75, 85
Brown, W.S. 101
Bunyan, J. 141
Burkhardt, M.A. 101
Burnard, P. 102

Carlsmith, J.M. 114
Chriss, J.J. 86
Clark, T.E. 102
Cobb, J.B. 85
Collins-Mayo, S. 101
Collinson, S.I. 46, 51
Come, A.B. 101
Conger, J.J. 28, 33

Conn, J.W. 35
Conran, T. 102
Covey, S.R. 102
Crabb, L. 26, 32, 35, 46
Cray, G. 101
Cupach, W.R. 126

Davis, C. 126, 127
Davis, R. 86
Denton, E.A. 97
Diamond, J. 142
Drakeford, D. 86
Drane, J. 101
Duck, S.W. 120, 126
Duffy, S.J. 126
Dunlop, M.V. 20

Ellens, J.H. 28, 33, 34
Ellison, H.L. 98
English, A.C. 142
English, H.B. 142
Erikson, E.H. 28, 29, 33, 114
Etzioni, A. 102

Festinger, L. 114
Field, A. 44, 51
Finn, T.M. 43, 50
First, M.B. 115
Ford, D.F. 110, 114
Foster, R. 19
Fouch, R.E. 102

Fowler, J.W. 29, 34, 35
Freud, S. 28, 33
Frost, R. 85
Fullan, M. 97, 102
Furedi, F. 77, 86

Gibson, T.L. 86
Gilligan, C. 28, 33
Gleitman, H. 114, 115
Goldbrunner, J. 77, 85
Goleman, D. 29, 33, 68, 102, 142
Gotz, I.L. 115
Goudie, N. 85
Greene, T.A. 127
Groeschel, B. 34
Gross, J. 85
Gunn, G. 102

Haring, B. 35, 114
Hay, D. 96, 101
Henderson, D.M. 77, 86
Hess, C.R. 142
Holmes, P.R. xvi, xx, 16, 19, 41, 43,
    50, 51, 85, 127
Hughes, H. 85
Hunt, K. 96, 101
Hurding, R. 77, 86

Izzard, S. 102

Jacobs, J.M. 35
Janov, A. 29, 33
Johnson, E.L. 101
Jung, C.J. 28, 33

Kao, C.C.L. 35
Keating, T. 35
Kiefer, C.W. 107, 114
Koenig, H.G. 102

Lambourne, R. 111, 114
Lapierre, L.L. 126, 127
le Dioux, J. 142
le Peau, A. 85
Lee, J.Y. 111, 114, 126

Levinson, D.J. 34
Ling, T. 126, 127

MacMullen, R. 44, 51
Malony, H.N. 101
Marshall, I. 101
Martin, P. 51
Martsolf, D.S. 94, 98, 101
May, R. 86
Mayo, B. 101
McFadyen, A. 108, 114
McGrath, A.E. 58, 68
Menninger, K. 114
Merton, T. 34
Mickley, J.R. 94, 98, 101
Middlemiss, D. 33
Miller, M.E. 35, 101
Mitroff, I.I. 97
Moon, G.W. 86
Moore, R.L. 127
Murphy, N. 101

Nagai-Jacobson, M.G. 101
Nee, W. 19
Nicholson, K. 101
Nygren, A. 85

O'Connor, T.J. 102
Oden, T.C. 74, 85
Offner, H. 19

Pease, A. 29, 34
Pease, B. 34, 39
Peck, M.S. 29, 34
Peterson, E.H. 86
Philip, J. 34
Piaget, J. 28, 33
Popkes, W. 77, 86
Price, C.W. 16, 19
Pryor, R.J. 101
Purton, A.C. 101

Quinn, R.E. 29, 34

Rahner, K. xix, xx, 60, 68
Regan, D. 51

Reid, M.A. 4
Robb, J.H. 101
Roberts, R.C. 9
Robinson, J.A.T. 114
Roof, W.C. 97, 102
Ross, A. 126
Rupp, G. 86

Sanders, J.O. 30, 34
Savage, S. 101
Schaeffer, F.A. 98, 102
Schermer, V.L. 102
Schippers, R. 30, 34
Schwartz, R.C. 102
Shafranske, E.P. 34, 85
Shelton, R.L. xx
Skarsaune, O. 43, 50
Spitzberg, B.H. 126
Steere, D.A. 102
Strong, A.H. 114

Thomas, F.A. 35
Thompson, M. 102
Twelftree, G. 50

Underhill, E. 51

Van Kaam, A. 35
van Peursen, C.A. 101
Via, D.O. 122, 126, 127

Wade, C.R. 19
Wesley, J. 27, 78
White, J. 16, 19
Wiersbe, W. 34
Wilber, K. 34
Wiley, T. 114
Wilhoit, J.C. 34
Wilkinson, J. 46, 50
Willard, D. 46, 51
Williams, S.B. xvii, xx, 14, 19, 51, 85
Wood, J.T. 114
Woodbridge, P.D. 114
Wright, N.G. 126

Young-Eisendrath, P. 35, 101

Zohar, D. 101

Scripture Index

Genesis
1:1   11
2:7   76, 93
2:27   76
3:1–4   120
6:5   121
8:21   121
17:9ff.   108
18:1ff.   11
18:10   11
18:27   76
22:15   108
37:19   100

Exodus
15:26   16, 43, 140
20:4–5   123
33:5   107
34:6–7   123

Leviticus
26:1ff.   108

Deuteronomy
28:61   27
30:15–20   16

Joshua
5:13–15   11

1 Kings
11:1ff.   110

1 Chronicles
21:4–8   124

Job
34:14–15   76

Psalms
32:8–9   107
42:10   124
55:19   107, 109
85:8–9   111
90:3   76
94:19   100
127:1   132

Psalms/Psalter   100

Proverbs
5:22   108

Isaiah
6:3–7   3
52:13–53:12   11
59:1–2   124

Jeremiah
2:10–13   120
7:26   43
17:1   120
17:9–10   120

Lamentations
5:7   123

Ezekiel
18:19–20   124

Daniel
2:3   100

Matthew
1:20   100
2:18   23
3:25   132
4:17   108
5:48   4
7:7–8   132
8:20   50
10:8   81
10:26–27   124
12:31   108
12:33   8
12:44   132
18:3   xvii, 43, 113
18:20   62
22:39   4
26:69–75   124
27:50   76
28:19   46

Luke
5:1   50
5:8   3

6:43	8	7:14–20	121	5:11	7
9:2	81	7:15	112	5:17	14
9:57–62	50	7:19	7	6:6	7
10:25–28	7	8:1ff	147	9:11	7
10:27	5	8:18	148	9:13	7
11:24–26	32	8:29	43	12:9	30
11:43	23	10:5–21	110		
17:19	50	12:1	4, 100	**Galatians**	
19:45ff.	138	12:3	122	2:20	110
24:46–47	108	12:4–5	63	5:17	112
		12:6	100	5:22–23	8
John		12:7	100	5:23	8
1:12–13	83	12:8	100	5:24–26	8
4:24	100	12:13	4, 7	6:7	124
5:14	112	12:18	7		
8:34	113	15:19	100	**Ephesians**	
11:33	138			1:14	4
11:35	138	**1 Corinthians**		1:17–19	65
13:35	5	2:6	30	3:6–8	100
14:15ff.	15	3:16	4	3:19	65
14:20–21	3	4:14ff.	100	4:11	100
14:23–24	5	6:19	3, 4	4:13	43
14:25–27	139	7:7–8	100	4:15, 25	7
14 – 17	3	11:27ff.	27	4:25	63
15:2	8	12:1ff.	66	4:32	7
15:20	90	12:8	100	5:3	3
16:8–11	139	12:8–10	100	5:19	100
17:1ff.	62	12:9	100	6:18	100
17:22–24	xix	12:10	100		
		12:12–13	100	**Philippians**	
Acts		12:12ff.	62	1:20	8
2:17	100	12:27	63	2:3	7, 23
5:5ff.	27	12:28	100	2:5	13
6:1ff.	74	12:30	100	2:12	13
7:49	132	13:3	100	2:12–15	83
7:59	76	13:4	8	3:3	100
9:8	27	13:12	26	3:7–11	110
11:5ff.	107	14:14	100	3:10	65
16:6	100	14:20	30	3:12	13
		14:27–28	100	3:15	30
Romans		14:33	122	4:5	8
5:2–3	7			4:7	
5:3–4	8	**2 Corinthians**		4:11–12	
5:12–14	148	1:4–5	100		
6:23	108	4:16	112	**Colossians**	
7:4ff	8	5:6, 8	7	1:15–23	xviii

1:24–29	148	1:18	100	**James**	
1:27	36, 146	6:11	7	1:21	7, 27, 57
1:28	43			3:1–12	124
2:18	23			3:16	122
3:9	124	**2 Timothy**		5:16	62
3:11	146	2:20–22	132		
3:12	7	4:7	30		
3:13	8			**1 Peter**	
3:14	146	**Titus**		1:2	7
3:16	146	1:1	112	1:15–16	7
				2:1–2	57
1 Thessalonians				2:5–9	4
2:13	83	**Philemon**		4:9–10	100
5:18	7	10	100		
5:23	13, 58			**1 John**	
		Hebrews		3:2–3	26
1 Timothy		3:6	132	4:7–10	xix
1:2	100	5:13–14	27	4:11–12	147
1:12	66	12:10	62	4:20	148

Subject Index

1300s 48
1800s 74
20th century 75
21st century 47, 60, 63, 96–97, 139
4th century 44

abortion 31
abundance 54
abuse 31, 133
academic life 98
Adam 148
adaptability 40
approachability 40
addictions 75
    addictive habits 48
administration, gift of 100
almsgiving, gift of 100
American Psychological
    Association 75
anger 36, 133, 138
anguish 27
anointing 100
    prophetic 65
apostleship, gift of 100
approachability 40
Aquinas 48
arrogance 112
authentic
    community 63
    spirituality xviii, 92
avarice 112

baggage 93
    baggage list xviii
    emotional baggage 47
    naming our baggage 123
balance 15
balloon 137
band meetings 78
baptism 44
    in the Holy Spirit 100
becoming 94
    holy 3, 4
    more human xvi, 7, 57
    more pious 47
    more whole 75
behaviour patterns 4
being more real 112
believer – new xiv
Bible 47, 48, 57
    Biblical background 2
    Bible-based theology 120
    Biblical journey 5
    Biblical perspective 3
    Biblical Trinitarian context 15
    Biblical views of Christ-
        likeness xviii
biodiversity 97
biographies xvi
biology 96
biomedicine 79
birthday present 14

bitterness 47
blame culture 131
blueprint xvii
body 59
    disciplined in mind and body 40
Body of Christ xvii, 3–4, 62, 71
body-spirit unity 18, 76, 93, 119,
    132
book cover 2
bravery 36
burn-out 31, 47

Cappadocian Fathers xvi
car 2
    accident 133
    motor mechanics 97
Catechesis 43
    catechumen 43
Catholic ethic of holiness 78
celibacy, gift of 100
Celtic spirituality 98
change
    Christ-like change 111
    deep change 48
    discipleship change 84
    holistic change 67
    intentional change 18
    positive change xvii, 5, 16
    subliminal change 47
    therapeutic change 28, 48, 78, 98
character 1
    character-building 8
    studies xviii, ix
charismatic tradition 82
Chelsea Flower Show 97
children 43
Christ
    Christ's example 43
    Christ's leadership 43
    Christ's perspective 23
    Christ's teaching 43
    finished work of Christ 15
    fullness of Christ 81
    holiness of Christ 3
    how Christ lived 46
    person and work of Christ 11

Christ-centred 96
    abide in Christ 8
    apprentice of Christ 46
    as Lord 4
    as role model 5
    Body of Christ xvii, 3–4, 62, 71
    calling in Christ 8
    Christ in me xix, 3, 146
    Christ in us 5, 36
    Christ-like holiness 44
    clones of Christ 6
    confessing Christ 5
    disciples of Christ 5
    imitators of Christ 14
    indwelling of Christ 3
    intimacy with Christ 69
    Lordship of Christ 4
    mirror Christ 7
    relationship with Christ 108
    therapeutic knowing of Christ
      111
Christian
    books 57
    culture 44
    discipleship 46–47
    journey 46
    virtues 2, 7, 48
Christianity
    fundamentals of Christianity 117
    Hellenistic Christianity 77
Christ-likeness
    Biblical views of xviii
    contemporary views of Christ-
      likeness xviii
Church 3, 111
    church planter, gift of 100
    Early Church xv, 19, 42–43, 48, 58,
      74, 77
    outside the church 29
    sick list xiv
citizenship 145
class meetings 78
clinical
    approach 31
    model 31
    practice 96

comforting, gift of 100
communicate, ability to 88
community
   authentic community 63
   breakdown of community 97
   divine community xvii, 16
   therapeutic faith community
     xviii
comparative religions 29
compassion 7, 36
condemnation, feelings of 30
confessing Christ 5
confession 3
confessional Christianity 117
confidence 7
congregation 16
   congregational life 3
connectedness 95
connecting 94
consistency 37
consoling, gift of 100
Constantine 44
contemporary
   charismatic meeting 27
   Christian maturity 30
   people 99, 111
   psychological perspective 26
   society 139
   spirituality 96
   view of discipleship 47
   views of Christ-likeness xviii
   world xviii
contentment 7
contrition 112
control 40
convents 6
conversion 132
converts 46
   new converts 44
courage 8
created world xvi, 59
creativity 111
culture
   blame culture 131
   Christian culture 44
   health culture 82

damage 4
darkness 119
   darkness in us xviii
   others' darkness 37
David 78
decades
   think in decades 40
deceit 31
definitions of
   maturity 26
   disciple 46
delighting 145
demonic 95
   demonically distressed 27
denial 49, 65, 79
   live in denial 31
depravity 119
deprivation 54
desires 1
despair 31
destiny, sense of 70
developmental models 29
die, plan to die well 56
discerning 55
   discern good and evil 31
   discerning spirits, gift of 100
   discernment 65
discipleship xvi, 2, 48, 78, 84
   contemporary view of
     discipleship 47
   definition of disciple 46
   disciples of Christ 5
   discipleship change 84
   journey 148
   salugenic discipleship 83
   salugenic discipleship journey
     80
   therapeutic discipleship 50
   wholeness journey xvi
disciplined in mind and body
   40
disillusionment 47
diversity 61
divine community xvii, 16
DNA 60
do everything well 52

dogmatic 118
dough 2
dreamer, gift of 100
dreams 23
drives 112
DSM 112

Early Church xv, 19, 42–43, 48, 58, 74, 77
ecologically sensitive 144
educational discourse 97
ego psychology 28
Emmaus 146
emotion xix, 2, 29, 137
    emotional abuse 31
    emotional baggage 47
    emotional illness 47
    emotional life 49, 137
    emotional maturing 31
    emotional wholeness 47
    Hebrew view of emotion 138
    meeting Jesus emotionally 45
    toxic emotion 137
empowering 55
encouragement, gift of 100
enemies 82, 90
Enemy 1, 38
enjoy being yourself 22
enjoyable company 91
Enlightenment xvii, 48
EQ 96
eternal life xv
ethical leadership 97
Eucharist 47
Evangelical tradition 46, 78
evangelism 1
    gift of evangelism 100
Evil 119, 120, 127
    discern good and evil 31
executive 17
exercise 48, 49
    exercising spiritual gifting 104
exhortation, gift of 100
exorcisms 44
experience 45
eye 60

faith 7, 30
    development journey 47
    fact faith 45
    felt faith 44
    faith maturity 29
    gift of faith 100
faithfulness 8, 88
    in marriage 130
fallen damaged world 107
false self 141
family 128
    family life 52, 128
fasting 16, 17, 57
father 133
Father God 4, 31
fathering, gift of 100
fear
    of God 7, 72
    of intimacy 129
    of the Enemy 106
feeling
    is healing 137
    right feeling 83
feelings 45
    of self-condemnation 30
    of worthlessness 31
    bouquet of feeling 139
felt faith 44
Feng Shui 97
finger print 60
fishing 97
forbearance 8
forgiveness 7, 31
fortitude 7, 36
fragmentation 77
free will 110
fruit 8
    first fruits 4
    fruitfulness 24
    of the Spirit 48, 77

garden design 97
Garden of Eden 120
gender 53
    continuum 36, 38
    distinctives 22, 53

gender (*continued*)
  studies 97
  uniqueness of gender 38
generosity 7
gentleness 7, 8
gifting 133
gifts of the Spirit 77
goals 52
God
  godly 58
  God's character 10
  God's image 6, 40
  hearing God's voice 71
  indifferent to God 46
  mutuality in the Godhead vii
  relationship with God 69
  transforming presence of God
    2
goodness 8
Gospel 50, 79, 111
gospel of salvation v
gratitude 7
Great Commission 70
Greek ideas 76
  Greek view of emotion 138
Ground Zero 98
guilt 1, 3, 30

habits 60
  addictive habit 48
hamartia 108
hate 112, 138
healing xviii, 43, 46, 62
  feeling is healing 137
  gift of healing 100
  journey 31, 74
health 46, 82
  culture 82
  health care 96
  health care professionals 49
healthy lifestyle 143
hearing God's voice 71
heavenly Father 4
Hebrew
  concept 93
  perspective 76

Hebrew (*continued*)
  view of emotion 138
  view of sin 107
Hellenistic Christianity 77
helping professions 83
helps, gift of 100
hidden sin 57
high intelligence 49
holiness 7, 62, 58, 137
  Catholic ethic of holiness 78
  Christ-like holiness 44
  new life of holiness 43
  of Christ 3
holistic xv, 18
  change 67
holy 3, 4
  people 3
Holy Spirit 1, 3, 147
  gifts of the Spirit 77
  spiritual gifting 66, 99
  baptism in the Holy Spirit 100
home 128
homework 80
honor 7, 88
honored by both sexes 91
hope 7
  eternal hope 112
hospitality 7
  gift of hospitality 100
housegroup 49
how-to 18
humanity 58
  become more human xvi, 7,
    57
  human make-up 93, 98
  human nature 18, 109, 119
  human spirit 93
  more fully human 46
  more human viii
  student of human nature 53
  transformed humanity 15
humility 7, 23, 38

idolatry 112
Ignatian spirituality 98
illness emotional illness 47

image of God 6, 11, 22, 40
  imago Dei 61, 76, 80, 107, 147
immunity 49
individualistic 3
  private individuality vii
individuation 28
inherited sin 123
intellect ix, 2
  intellectual life 116
  intellectual potential 117
intelligence
  IQ 96
  social intelligence 63
SQ 96
intentional change 18
intercession, gift of 100
interpretation of dreams, gift of 100
interpretation of tongues, gift of 100
intimacy with Christ 69
IQ 96
Israel 3

jealousy 138
Joseph 78
journey v, vi, 2, 3, 4, 6, 8, 14, 16, 17,
    25, 78, 84, 121
  Biblical journey 5
  Christian journey 46
  discipleship journey 148
  discipleship wholeness journey vi
  faith development journey 47
  healing journey 31, 74
  personal journey 81
  Rapha journey 81
  salugenic discipleship journey 80
  spiritual journey 31, 47, 74
  therapeutic journey 46
joy 7, 8
judging 55
Jung 7
justice 7

kindness 7, 8
Kingdom of God xv, 7, 60
  Kingdom building 82
  Kingdom values 7

kneading 2
  kneading dough 4, 16
knowledge (intellectual/spiritual),
    gift of 100
knowledge 65

language 111
  lost language 111
laziness 48
leadership
  Christ's leadership 43
  ethical leadership 97
  gift of leadership 100
learning about God 118
Levites 3
life cycle 28
lifestyle
  disorder 49, 123
  ecologically sensitive lifestyle 144
  healthy lifestyle 143
  infamous lifestyle 48
  integrated lifestyle 17
  itinerant lifestyle 50
listen to others 88
literature, love of 118
live a lie 49
live in denial 31
live maturely 54
living well 56
longitudinal approach 28
Lordship of Christ 4
lost language 111
love 5, 7, 8
  choice to love 7
  for people 87
  give and receive love 130
  love others 90
  love ourselves vi
  loving your body 22
Love vi, vii, 16, 36
  God is Love 62
  loved by God 45

majesty 36
man's perspective 53
management, gift of 100

manhood 53, 133
martyrdom 44
   gift of martyrdom 100
materialism 97
mature vii, 57
   emotionally mature 46
   emotional maturing 31
   spiritual maturing 31
   theology 112
   live maturely 54
maturity 7, 26, 28, 77
   contemporary Christian
     maturity 30
   defining maturity 26
   faith maturity 29
   in Christ 2
meaning 94
media 49
medication 49
meditation ix, 16, 134
   meditating 2
meekness 7, 36
meeting Jesus viii, 45
   meeting Jesus emotionally 45
meetings, attending 47
men 87
mental health movement 82
mental hospital 74
mercy, gift of 100
meta-analysis 29
Middle Ages 48
mind
   disciplined in mind and body 40
   mind-body dualism 93
miracles 42
   miracles, gift of 100
missionary, gift of 100
mistakes 80
monasteries 6, 48
monastic order 48
moral stature 43
more fully human 46
Moses 78
mother 133
   motherhood 6
motivation 1

MRI scan 64
music, gift of 100
mutuality in the Godhead vii
mystic movement 45
mystical Christianity 45

nacham 108
National Curriculum 97
natural world 144
neural pathway 64
neuroscience 64
New Age 18, 92, 98
new believer 43
new converts 44
new creation 11, 50, 58, 120, 146
new life of holiness 43
New Testament 3, 11, 46, 77
nursing 98

obedience 7, 8
obesity 49
Old Testament 3, 16, 77, 108
old-fashioned language 111
openness 117
   openness of spirit 105
original sin 110
others
   speaking well of others 55
   others' darkness 37
oven 2

pagan 44
Paris 48
passion 1
   passion to give life 87
passive 2
passivity 83
pastor 111
   gift of, 100
pastoral care vi
pathology 112
patience 8
Pauline theology 112
peace 7, 8, 21
   peaceableness 7
Pentecostalism 120

perichoretic 62, 109
  perichoretic union vii
perseverance 8
personal
  journey 81
  responsibility 81, 110
  uniqueness 59–61
personality 1, 7
person-centred psychological
  therapy 121
personhood vii
perspective
  Biblical perspective 5
  Christ's perspective 23
  contemporary psychological
    perspective 26
  Hebrew perspective 76
  man's perspective 53
  woman's perspective 53
Peter 78
Pharisees vi
physical abuse 31
pious 47
poetry, gift of 100
politically aware 144
positive change vii, 5, 16
  Christ-like change 111
possessing 145
postmodernity vii
poverty, voluntary, gift of 100
poverty 50
power 36
  gift of 100
praying 57
  prayer, gift of 100
preaching, gift of 100
pre-incarnate 11
pride 112
  righteous pride 24
priest 3, 4
private individuality vii
professional life 98
prophecies 57
  gift of 100
prophetic anointing 65
pruning 8

Psalms / Psalter, gift of 100
psychological 18
  contemporary psychological
    perspective 26
  psychological model vii
  person-centred psychological
    therapy 121
  psychological therapies 79, 82, 96,
    121
  psychologically informed 111
psychology 28, 60, 74, 112, 113
  borderlands 29
  ego psychology 28
  folk psychology 78
  psychology research 96
psychophysiology 49
psychosocial development 28
purity 7
put others first 88

Quaker spirituality 98
quiet times 49

rape 31
Rapha journey 81
  Rapha principle 140
realist 37
reconciliation vii
redeemed 146
Reformed 119
relational wholeness viii
relationality 59
relationship with Christ 108
relationship with God 69
relationships vii, 1, 82, 87, 128
reliability 37
religious journey 48
repent 137
  repentance 108, 112
repress 49
resilience 36
responsibilities 19
  personal responsibility 81, 110
  responsible eating 48
Retreat, The Retreat, York 74
right feeling 83

right living 83
right thinking 83
righteous pride 24
righteously offensive 90

sacramental practice 47
sacrifice 112
saliva 60
salugenic 84
    salugenic discipleship 83
    salugenic discipleship journey 80
salvation 14, 62, 110
sanctification vi, 4, 57, 62
saved 146
schooling 97
Scripture 1, 10, 57, 72, 93, 109, 132
second class 5
secularism 97
seer, gift of 100
self
    at ease within yourself 21
    enjoy being yourself 22
    false self 141
    feelings of self-condemnation 30
    love ourselves vi
    promote one's self 24
    true self 141
    self-actualization 7
    self-control 8
    self-deceit 31, 110, 121
    self-worth 23
self-help movement 28
    self-help books 18, 31, 75
selfism 77
servant-hood, gift of 100
serve 7
    service, gift of 100
    serving, gift of 100
sexual abuse 31
shepherding, gift of 100
shub 108
sickness, inviting sickness 49
signs, gift of 100
sin ix, 3, 4, 45, 47, 62, 93, 108, 110
    Hebrew view of sin 107
    idea of sin 107

sin (*continued*)
    inherited sin 123
    original sin 110
    hidden sin 57
    single sin 130
single 6
single parent 17
single-mindedness 110
sleep deprivation 49
smoking 49
social autism 64
social brain 63
social intelligence 63
social neuroscience 64
social Trinity, see Trinity
socially aware 144
society 111
    contemporary society 139
solitary sainthood 16
Solomon 110
song of the Lord, gift of 100
song-writing, gift of 100
sorry 41
sozo 50
spirit 59
    your spirit 105
spiritual abuse 31
spiritual beliefs 97
spiritual discipline 16
    spiritual disciplines 46, 48, 58
spiritual distress 96
spiritual gifting 66, 99
    spiritual gifts 48, 65
spiritual house ix, 132
spiritual journey 31, 47, 74
spiritual maturing 31
spiritual nature 92, 103
    spiritual health 96
spiritual virtue ix
spiritual world 137
    spiritual reality 92, 93, 103
spirituality 29, 46, 94
    authentic spirituality viii, 92
    contemporary spirituality 96
    intangible spirituality 99
    our spirituality 103

spirituality (*continued*)
  Quaker spirituality 98
  spirituality movement 63
  traditional Christian
    spirituality 48
  transforming spirituality 57, 98
SQ 96
stage model 29
  stage development 77
  stages of development 28
state religion 44
stereo-types 36
street drugs 49
student of human nature 53
study group 16
study theology 48
subliminal change 47
suffering 73, 112

TB patients 78
teachable spirit 116
teaching theology 48
teaching, gift of 100
tears 36, 45
temperament 36
temperance 7
temples of God 4
temptation, resist 107
tender-heartedness 118
theology
  Bible-based 120
  mature theology 112
theophanies 11
theoretical physics 97
therapeutic 44, 79, 81
  change 28, 48, 78, 98
  discipleship 50
  faith community viii
  introspection 78
  journey 46
  knowing of Christ 111
  psychological therapies 79, 82, 96,
    121
  wholeness 84
therapists 74, 111
thorny issues 11

tongues, gift of 100
Torah 116
totus homo 76
toxic pasts 79
training
transcendence 94
transformation 15, 80
  transformative 64
  transformed automatically 14
  transformed humanity 15
  transforming presence of God 2
  transforming spirituality 57, 98
Trinity vi, vii, ix, 15, 62, 109
  social Trinity 64, 66, 69, 83, 94,
    132
  Trinitarian context 15
triumphalist 81
trustworthiness 37
truthfulness 7
typology 36

unconquerable spirit 105
union with Christ 43, 77
unique 6
  personhood 61
  our own uniqueness 17
  personal uniqueness 59–61
  uniqueness of gender 38
universities 48
uxoriousness 110

value 94
verbal abuse 31
virtues ix, 77
  Christian virtues 2, 7, 48
visionary, gift of 100

wealth-creating, gift of 100
well-being 82
Wesley, John 27, 78
Western Christianity 76
Western Church vii
Western culture 98
whole vii, 75
wholeness vi, viii, 30, 43, 48, 74, 80,
    82, 84, 110

wholeness (*continued*)
   discipleship wholeness journey vi
   emotional wholeness 47
   relational wholeness viii
   therapeutic wholeness 84
windows 133
wine 8
wisdom 7
   wisdom, gift of 100
wiser 29
witchcraft 95
women iii, 6, 87
   womanhood 53, 133
   woman's perspective 53

world
   created world vi, 59
   fallen damaged world 107
   natural world 144
   things of the world 58
worship, gift of 100
worthlessness 31
wrong 117

Yahweh 3, 107
your spirit 105
yourself
   enjoy being yourself 22
   at ease within yourself 21

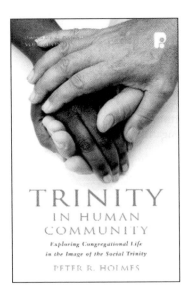

Trinity in Human Community

Exploring Congregational Life in the Image of the Social Trinity

Peter R. Holmes

God is a community of love and so relationship lies at the very heart of God's identity. In this book Peter Holmes builds on growing interest in idea of the Trinity as a divine 'society' by offering a *practical application* to congregational life. The central issue is *how faith community could better reflect the harmony and diversity of the Trinity*. Holmes suggests a number of practical principles intended to help local congregations implement at a personal and communal level what it means to love and worship the Trinity within authentic human faith community.

'Many church leaders are struggling with the demands of contemporary church community. Yet many of us never stop to ask significant questions about what congregational life is, what God wants it to be, and how it should relate to our contemporary understanding of community. A very thought-provoking and, at times, disturbing read.' – **Rev Dr Rob Frost**, Director of Share Jesus International

'This is a *must read* for all who want their congregations to be a place where people from many and diverse background feel at home because their Church community mirrors an excitingly dynamic divine Trinity-in-community.' – **Dr Knut Heim**, lecturer in Old Testament, The Queen's Foundation, Birmingham

Peter R. Holmes is a management trainer and co-founder of Christ Church Deal in Kent and Rapha. He is a member of the Association of Therapeutic Communities.

978-1-84227-470-5